This book is dedicated to Frank and Peaches.
I love you.

Table of Contents

TWO DREAMS

Trampoline Dream

WHEN I WAS FIRST diagnosed with Cushing's disease, a few months in, when I was still reeling from the newness of it all, I had a dream that I was at a party. Outside, in the dark, was a trampoline. It was one of those hot Portland nights, when it's in the 80s until well after midnight. People were milling around with their beers, men had their shirts unbuttoned to the navel. Those brave enough to go barefoot were squishing the ashy dust between their toes and flexing their dehydrated calves up and down, up and down. Women ran their bony fingers through curly hair, feeling the sweat near their scalps and the napes of their necks. The house was a thin, white, wooden structure with dark upstairs windows and a dim glow from the kitchen. Its bony white walls were throwing back some of the moonlight at us. Tiki torches kept a few straggling mosquitoes at bay. And we were all watching a group of young women jumping up and down on a trampoline.

One of them, a thin blonde, was saying something about fat people. Throwing the word out of her mouth like the word rapist, or bigot, or idiot. I dragged her down from the trampoline, and she was screaming and trying to fight back, but I was bigger and stronger than her. And I started strangling her. Of course, when I woke up I realized this woman was me. I had never had a dream like that. I had often seen them portrayed in movies. Like a dream with smoke machines and dwarves, it seemed so clichéd. But it served its purpose—to show me that my old self, my healthy self, was gone forever and I'd be a fool to want her back.

Fourth of July Dream

LAST NIGHT I DREAMT it was the Fourth of July. In the dream, my friends and I are sitting on the edge of a canyon, waiting for the fireworks to begin. It dawns on me that we're looking across the canyon at my family's old property in Corbett. Our five acres. There's the white, double-wide mobile home, the scattered outbuildings, the broken bicycles, and the retired pickups.

From where we sit, my family seems to be bumping into each other blindly, then spinning away, flagellating like microorganisms under a microscope. They're having a barbeque. Someone pokes at the coals with the tongs, puts the tongs down, someone else picks them up, pokes at the hot dogs, puts them down. Every action is done then undone. Beers are kicked over half-drunk and small fountain fireworks knocked over, sending ash and sulfur over the gravel. One dog tries to mount another, gives up, and goes back to digging halfheartedly at the overgrown box garden. Firecrackers hit the ground in half-moon orbits.

If I squint, I can see Uncle Paul in a folding lawn chair, the plastic kind that sticks to your ass and breaks constantly. He's trying to get the seat to go back, but keeps hunching further and further forward. I can make out Aunt Linda's bad perm like a curly helmet around her skull; she's suddenly and awkwardly pulling down her pink sweatpants, revealing the even pinker shorts she wears underneath "just in case it gets too hot." Next to the ratty ferns and dwarf rhododendron bush Mom and Dad talk to Grandpa Ev while he tugs on a Camel Straight. The kids chase puppies with sparklers, and the puppies scatter, yapping in fear. Everyone's eating hot dogs and lifting dripping soda cans out of coolers. And everyone's bickering. None of them think they're bickering, they just think they're talking to each other, but to my friends it's obvious that something's about to blow up. Aunt Linda puts her pants back on as the sun passes behind a cloud.

In the dream, as my friends and I sprawl above the canyon, I begin to realize that we've assembled here to watch my family's fireworks. *Those people*, my friends are thinking, *they'll set off the fireworks, and we'll sit back and watch.*

And in the dream, none of my friends know that *those people* are my family, that I belong on the other side of the canyon. They don't know that I come from *those people*, the kind of people that didn't go to college, had kids at sixteen, had kids at twenty-one, had seven kids. The distance between my friends and my family is only an acre or so, but we might as well be on a distant planet.

I know in my heart that I need to be over there with them. But if I cross the canyon my friends will know. I'll be discovered for the spectacle that I am.

Cheese Clerk

I WORK IN THE cheese department of a busy, upscale grocery store. We sell around $3,000 worth of cheese a day. If you figure the average price of cheese is about $5 a piece, that means we sell 600 pieces of cheese a day. I personally cut, wrap, price, and label about a quarter of that. That means I wrap about 150 pieces of cheese a day. Multiply that by the four days a week I work and you get the figure of 600 pieces a week.

I can do this work with my eyes closed. I can cut, slice, and wrap cheese with the precision of a machine. While I work, it's possible for me to hold long conversations with actual people, or if no one else is around, the people in my mind. Customers come in with their cheese problems, questions, and complaints. Sometimes I can help them.

"Can I help you find a cheese?" I say.

"I'm having friends over tonight and I want this certain cheese but I don't remember the name," the woman replies.

"Can you describe it?"

"Well, let me think ... it was Italian and was kind of like a Parmesan but fruitier."

"Was it the Piave Vecchio?"

"Yes! That was it."

And I feel good. But often I can't help customers—we don't

have what they're looking for. Or, as is often the case, they don't really know what they want. Something sharp *and* spreadable? (It doesn't exist.) Something to use in place of a Cheddar in macaroni and cheese, but that has flavor—but not too much flavor? I sigh and try to be helpful. But sometimes I can only point them in the general direction of a good melter (Fontina, Gruyere) or something their in-laws from Michigan will like (Cotswold?). They leave, not dissatisfied necessarily, but confused, almost melancholy.

My job wears on me, but it's not dealing with customers that's hard, it's the fact that I have to stand in one place for eight hours a day twisting my arms and bending down to pick up wheels of cheese over and over until I have shooting back pain and tingling in my extremities. One summer my arms started going numb. More specifically, the ring and pinkie finger on my right hand. Sometimes, especially if I'd been on my bike for any length of time, my entire hand and arm would completely lose feeling. It'd take hours for it to come back and sometimes the persistent tingling would never completely go away.

I started to feel like my job was killing me. My back hurt all the time, and now, to make matters worse, I couldn't feel my fingers. One of the cheese managers at another store had recently come down with an extremely rare bacterial infection in his spine. It ate away some of his vertebrae, he could barely walk, and he'd almost died. The doctors told him that it was very rare, there were only a couple known cases worldwide, and they had no idea how he'd gotten it. But one thing that all these cases had in common was that everyone who'd been infected had worked with dairy. All of us cheese workers whispered under our breath that it must've been the cheese.

Another one of our managers was allergic to the sanitizer we used for our cheese-cutting equipment. She had to continually apply an anti-inflammatory cream to her hands. The backs of them were covered by flakes and scabs.

Yet another manager went to the doctor and found that his cholesterol was so high that he would have to be put on medication if he didn't change his diet. Still another manager, who was fond of saying that "you can eat as much cheese as you like as long as you eat fruit," found out he had diverticulitis.

As is often the case with me, I started complaining about my numb hands to anyone who would listen. Finally, a friend of my parents told me to stop complaining and go to the doctor. He was right. It could be something serious. My sister Sarah told me it was probably the beginning of carpal tunnel syndrome. She'd got it from bartending and had had similar symptoms. The woman who worked at the coffee shop across the street from my house told me she'd had carpal tunnel and had to have surgery. "It was very simple," she said, knocking the basket out of the espresso machine with one deft move of her wrist. "Snip snip, and I was cured." My mother was convinced my back was going out.

I went to the doctor and found out that it was nothing. I told my grandfather about it and he told me that he'd had the same symptoms for a year before they went away. And my numb fingers did eventually heal themselves.

Now, years later, I deal with a strange electro-shock sensation that runs down my right arm every time I move a piece of cheese from the scale to the cart we use for stocking. My knees crack every time I squat down. My lower back aches. But if this job didn't create such strange disturbances in the body, any respite from them wouldn't be so appreciated. I savor these breaks from pain in whatever form they appear to me. I squat behind the cheese case to clean a knife in the bucket of sanitizer. My knees crack on the way down and I feel the stretch along my calves and hamstrings. The feeling is beautiful and quiet. I pause here, my body frozen, half-crouched down where no one can see me. I let myself rest for 30 seconds until I hear a voice wafting over the case.

"Can I talk to someone who knows something about cheese?"

Bagel

IT'S 8:00 A.M. A man walks up to me in the cheese section and these are the first words I hear this morning: "If I were a bagel and I didn't want anyone to find me, where would I be?"

I stop what I'm doing and look up. "Well, if you were a bagel and you didn't want anyone to find you, you wouldn't be in the bakery, but that's where you are."

The man just looks at me confused.

"The bagels are in the bakery," I say.

He frowns and walks away.

Fontina

"I FOUND A FLY in my cheese," the woman says, handing me a bag across the counter. "I just thought you should know."

Sure enough, there it is, half-encased in a wedge of Italian Fontina. It must've flown into the still-hardening cheese and drowned there. Well, there are worse ways to die than drowning in cheese. "Do you want your money back?" I say.

The woman frowns and shakes her head. "I just thought you should know," she says.

It bothers me when customers do this. Just take the money. "It's not a big deal," I say. "Are you sure you don't want your money back?"

"I just thought you should know there was a fly in your cheese." She crosses her arms.

I look down at the bag of cheese. So now it's MY cheese. That's the way it always works. I feel like telling the woman that I don't make cheese, I just cut it and wrap it, and even if I did there'd be nothing I could do to prevent this little guy from flying into my warehouse, landing in my cheese, and dying. And even if I were to call up the distributor and ask where they buy the cheese, and then I were to call the Italian cheese-makers and complain about the flies, they'd just shrug and tell me "Tough Titty." Or something like that. I don't speak Italian.

Entry Level Goat Cheese

"I'm LOOKING FOR an entry level goat cheese," the man says to me. He has some flour tortillas and a couple of chicken breasts in his shopping cart. He looks worried.

I wonder what an "entry level goat cheese" is. I know what a goat is. I know what cheese is. Goat cheese is the result of a process. It's what happens when grass interacts with a goat, its hormones, a farmer, mold, and time. It's what happens when a bodily fluid is exposed to extremes in temperature, to centuries-old traditions and the market economy. Goat cheese is the result of an accident eons ago when early herding cultures started milking their goats and left some of the milk in a leather sack overnight, hanging from the eave of their hut, or in the corner of their cave. Goat cheese is what happens when you age the goat's milk, then wrap it in wax, in leaves, or esophageal tubing. I know what this is.

But what is entry level? The point at which you enter? Where the grass enters mouths, stomachs, udders? Is it where the milk enters the world, hot and steaming from the teat? Is it where I enter the grocery store, enter my employee number into the time clock and don my hat, nametag, and apron? Is the entry level where the wire enters the cheese, splitting it in two? Is it where the cheese enters the plastic wrap, and gets entered into the scale at $15.99 a pound? Is entry level the place where I spend eight hours a day cutting, wrapping, weighing, and pricing the byproduct of an animal? The result of a process that begins and ends with digestion, that begins with the earth and ends with the earth? Is it where I package my own bodily fluids, my blood, sweat, and tears into eight-hour shifts, ten-minute breaks, and two-week pay periods?

I look at the man, his face impatient, eager to suckle at the teat of my vast cheese knowledge. I feel like telling him that every entry level is also an exit level. That all hierarchy is an illusion. That he should follow his heart. Instead I recommend the Goat Gouda, the Goat Jack, or if he's in the mood for something saltier, the Murcia Curado.

My Vast Cheese Knowledge

1. MY FAVORITE GROCERY STORE joke goes like this. A man walks up to the register and unloads his basket. He slaps down some Hungry Man TV dinners, single serving ice cream tubs, a toilet paper four-pack, a single serving of macaroni salad, and one apple. The cashier looks at his groceries and says, "You must be single."

The man looks up and says, "Can you tell because of what I'm buying?"

"No. I can tell because you're ugly."

2. We sell the most string cheese on Sunday nights.

3. Because of their longer commutes, suburbanites have less free time. They're also more likely to have expensive nail jobs that they don't want ruined by crumbling up Gorgonzola. The store will charge them on average about a dollar extra per pound to pour Gorgonzola from a five-pound bag into small tubs so that they don't have to touch the cheese, so that all they have to do is open the plastic container and pour it into their salad bowls, dress the salads, toss, and consume. A dollar per pound so that besides the cow's intestinal and mammary parts, not to mention the liberal amount of microorganisms in the blue cheese mold, the only things that will touch their Gorgonzola will be made of steel and plastic.

The company we buy the crumbled Gorgonzola from charges us about 50 cents extra a pound. Sounds like a bum deal until you remember that the cows work for free.

4. I am working in the cheese department with my back to the counter. I hear a man and a woman talking about cheese at the cheese case.

"Do you want to get a Camembert?" the man asks.

"No."

"How about some Oregon Blue?"

"You know what I like?" she says. "I like the Gorgonzola that is already crumbled."

Silence.

The woman speaks again. "By the look on your face I can tell that you think that's not very good."

"It's just that what I like isn't the same as what you like. It's not better or worse, it's just taste."

From this I can tell that the two of them haven't been dating very long.

5. A man walks up to the cheese case and says, "I was in Spain a month ago and I had this really good cheese called Queso. Do you have it?"

6. A woman walks up to the case and says, "I was in France a year ago and we had this really good cheese called Fromage. Do you have it?"

7. Women say, "I can't find the cream cheese."

Men say, "If I were looking for the cream cheese, where would I find it?"

8. Three men walk up to the counter. One of them points to the

Flora Nell blue cheese and says, "Look! That cheese is named after me!" He looks up at me. "Is this good?"

"The Flora Nell? Yes, it *is* good."

"Oh. Flora Nell. I thought it was Flora Neil. You should have said Flora Neil. You could've gotten a sale."

"I thought your name was Nell," I say.

"I am looking for an Italian cheese," says one of the other men. "It was creamy—"

"Fontina?" I ask.

"No."

"Was it a brie?"

"No."

"Taleggio?"

"Yes! Fellatio!"

"Taleggio?" I say again.

9. I am trying to sell goat cheese with Oregon hazelnuts and Frangelico. I offer two women small samples. Their eyes close and their heads tip back slightly. "Oh my God! It's like cheese ice cream! Where can I find it?"

I show them where it's located in the case. Both of them pick it up and put it in their baskets.

A man walks up and is browsing the cheese case.

"Do you want to try something fabulous while you're browsing?" I ask. The man nods and I hand him a sample of the Frangelico cheese.

He puts the sample in his mouth as I describe the cheese to him. His face suddenly turns sour. "It's sweet," he says, as if I've just given him a sample of his own semen. He spits the cheese into his palm and walks away in disgust.

11. I offer the old woman with the mustache a sample of the French triple cream Delice de Bourgogne.

"I love this creamy cheese," she says. "Hard cheese really stops up my bowels."

I don't think I've heard her right. "I'm sorry. Hard cheese what?"

The woman licks the taster spoon and smiles at me. "IT STOPS UP MY BOWELS!"

"Oh," I say. "Interesting."

"After World War Two," she continues, "I went out and bought a huge block of Tillamook cheese. During the war we couldn't buy that stuff without stamps. Anyway I ate the whole thing. I've never been the same since."

Two hours later an old man walks up to the case and I give him a sample of the Cabot Clothbound Cheddar. "That is so good," he says.

"Isn't that amazing?" I say.

I give him a sample of Shaft's Bleu Vein.

"This is so tempting," he says as he puts the cheese in his mouth. "But I shouldn't be eating cheese."

"Why not?" I ask. Why do I always ask?

"Because it makes my skin break out right here." The man points to the space between his very bushy eyebrows.

Two women approach the cheese case with two children. They taste some eight-month Manchego from the counter and I offer them some Delice de Bourgogne. The older woman loves it. "This is so good!" she says. "Where is this in the case?"

I point it out for her.

"Boy, that is good cheese. How much salt is in that cheese?"

"I don't know," I say. "Probably a lot. You know, your best bet is Swiss cheese or a reduced sodium cheese."

"I'm a diabetic and on chemo," the woman says. "I'm not supposed to have a lot of salt. Those reduced salt cheeses are usually pretty awful."

"I know," I say.

Book Club Cheese

A COUPLE YEARS AGO, when my mother first started attending a book club, she asked me to pick out some cheeses and give a little talk on them when it was her turn to host the meeting. The ladies were impressed, or at least they acted as if they were. Several years later, my aunt (who is in the same book club) called in a panic from Trader Joe's wanting to know what I would recommend now that it was her turn to host. Over a spotty cell phone connection, I coached her through the Trader Joe's cheese section. I talked her into a Manchego. She acted as though I'd just helped her perform brain surgery. "Martha!" she said. "You're a lifesaver!"

A couple months later I'm cutting cheese while a woman browses the case. She starts grunting and throws the brie down in disgust. "Do you have Delice de Bourgogne?"

"No, but we have this one. It's very similar," I say, pointing out another triple cream.

The woman ignores me and starts scanning the case as if she's looking for the wire to cut to a ticking time bomb. "It's my book club tonight!" she says. "You guys don't have any of the cheeses I need!" She picks up a Camembert only to drop it half-heartedly. It rolls on top of the Red Dragon.

"Well, if you'd like to taste anything, let me know," I say cheerfully.

She ignores my offer and frowns. "Is this good?" She holds up a cave-aged Gruyere.

"It's great."

The woman places it in her basket.

"What book are you discussing tonight?" I ask.

She doesn't look up. *"Angel Fire."*

"Hmm, never heard of it." I continue wrapping cheese.

The woman is rifling through the Scottish cheddars and I realize this is probably not the best thing to say. She groans again in frustration, throws a piece of cheese down, and walks away in a huff.

Later that day I go home thinking about the stress surrounding book clubs, how women are often more interested in impressing each other with their hosting abilities then they are in discussing the book. As a lover of books and writing, this irks me. But as a lover of cheese, I should be okay with it—right? And I wonder— what kept me from telling the woman at the cheese counter that I am a writer? That I am writing a book?

I have spent over half my life serving people, starting as a dishwasher when I was fifteen. In the past fifteen years I've been a busser, a hostess, a waitress, a cocktail server, a deli worker, a prep cook, and now a cheese clerk. Rule number one of the service industry is the same thing they tell nurses in nursing school: don't talk about yourself to the patient. In other words, people are coming to you to ask your expert opinion about cheese or their blood pressure or whatever—they're not coming to you to get to know you as a three-dimensional human being. They don't care who you are.

Until I worked with a certain woman at a busy Italian restaurant in my early twenties, I'd always taken it for granted that everyone knew this rule. She was my own age but had never worked in a restaurant before. She'd just graduated from college with a degree in English and dance.

One night after work, she and I went out for a drink to commiserate. "I'm running around pouring people water," she said, "and clearing their plates and everything, and it's like—they don't know anything about me. They don't know I'm really a dancer."

I stared at her for a minute and took another sip of beer. "You don't want them to know that," I said.

"But they look at me and think I'm just a hostess. That that's all I am."

"Honey," I said, feeling for the first time like a veteran of the service industry, "that knowledge is what's yours to keep. That's your treasure. Keeping that private is the only way you're going to keep from going crazy." And it's true: if you can't deal with this, you might not last long serving people. In the customer service world, in the world of giving the most of yourself away on a daily basis, there's this paradox where in the end, you really give people the least. You become a cut-out of yourself. You have neither great loves nor great hates. You are not a hater of Cotswold—you are just not a "fan" of Cotswold. You do not confess that you would give your left arm for a vacation in France, you only say that your customer's week in the wine country sounds "fantastic."

And so, I wonder, in the case of the book club cheese, with my own book finally coming out, will I break my own rule and tell customers that I am really a writer? That this cheese gig is only my day job? That they should care more about the book than the cheese? Or maybe I should be taking advantage of the fact that people care so much about cheese? I mull this over all day. As I label the Oscar Wilde Aged Irish Cheddar, his musing face stares out at me. "Look what they do," he whispers. "You die in a gutter and they put your face on a piece of cheese."

When I get home from work I ask my boyfriend if he thinks people would pay to have an in-home tasting and seminar on cheese. "Taught by me," I say hopefully.

"I don't think so, honey," he says.

FRANK

Lunch with Frank

THE FIRST TIME I went to lunch with my grandfather Frank I was twenty-three. It wasn't that we didn't get along, it was just that he had never been a part of my life. He was only sixteen when my father was born. He and my grandmother Peaches had only stayed married for a total of six months.

Frank took me to The Black Angus. Before we went into the restaurant, Frank pointed up at the large neon sign. "When I was going to school in Eugene, we used to go here for lunch. The 'G' was burnt out in the sign."

It was noon on a weekday in Eugene, Oregon. There was hardly anyone else in the restaurant. The special was ground sirloin. Frank asked the waitress if the meat was ground on the premises.

"What do you mean?"

"I mean, do you get the meat in a big hunk and grind it here? Or do you get it already ground up into steaks?"

"It's already ground up," said the waitress.

"Well I don't want that. I'll have the salmon. And a glass of red wine."

"What kind of red wine would you like? We have Cabernet, Merlot—"

"That sounds good."

"Which one?"

"Red."

"The Cabernet?"

"Fine."

I ordered a hamburger. After the waitress walked away, Frank explained that he'd stopped eating ground meat because he'd heard how the meat came from a bunch of different cows, and how there was probably shit in the meat all ground up together. He held up his hand. "I don't judge you for getting a hamburger, though," he said.

When the wine came, Frank swallowed it all in one gulp. "I hate the taste of red wine," he said.

"Then why did you order it?"

"It's good for you to have one glass of red wine a day. It's good for your heart. I also eat a handful of walnuts every day."

Frank told me he didn't like walnuts, either, but they were also supposed to be good for you.

As we ate, Frank described his special diet to me. "Every night I boil vegetables till they are soft. I eat the vegetables, and then I drink the water I boiled them in. Vegetables lose some of their vitamins when you boil them. So I drink the water to get some of the vitamins back."

After lunch, I excused myself to have a cigarette outside. Frank paid the bill and came out and leaned against the siding. "You know," he said, "you can tell me anything you want. Just because I'm an old man it doesn't mean you can't tell me about drugs. I don't care. I used to do some of that myself, you know."

For a moment, I wished I did have some crazy drug story to tell Frank, but I didn't. I couldn't figure out what exactly he wanted, anyway. I knew that Frank had worked at the women's prison in Salem for 30 years before he retired. Maybe he thought all young people were into using drugs. We got in the car and he started to drive me home. He asked me what my favorite movies were. I said that one of my all-time favorite musicals was *West Side Story*.

"I hate that movie!" he said.

"Why?"

"Because it takes something serious, like gang violence, and turns it into a joke, with everyone singing and dancing around." He rolled his eyes.

"I guess I've never thought about it that way," I said.

"What's your favorite musical?" I asked.

"*Chicago.*"

A couple months later, Frank and I went to the only Indian restaurant in Eugene and I asked him about TV shows. It turned out he was still very traditional when it came to gender roles. He told me that he didn't like the TV show *Voyager*, the *Star Trek* spin-off, because the ship had a female captain. "It just didn't seem realistic," he said.

"What shows do you like?" I asked.

"What's that one called? *Love and Marriage? Babies in a Baby Carriage?*"

"You mean *Married with Children?*"

"That's the one. I love that show!"

About a year and a half later, Frank and my grandmother re-married after a 50-year separation. Frank moved in with my grandma in Gresham, and didn't visit me in Eugene as often. Soon I had to share him with all my other siblings. He started playing chess with my brother on Wednesdays. Simone, my little sister, played pool with him on Mondays. He babysat my sister Ana's kids and went out to dinner with my parents on a nearly weekly basis. He even got a huge painting commissioned of him and Simone playing pool. It hangs in his living room next to the family portraits: Frank and Peaches at sixteen, fresh-faced and grinning in the snow of Mt. Hood; Frank and his deceased wife, Anne; Frank's son, Alex, outside their house in Salem; Frank with a full head of hair; Frank bald with a beard; and finally, the portrait of him and my grandmother taken shortly after their second wedding. Frank is grinning.

"I look like the vice-principal of a grade school in that one," he says.

Interview with Frank

WHAT FOLLOWS is an interview I conducted several years after Frank and Peaches re-married. It began as a conversation about jobs, as a way to get to know my new / old grandfather. But there were some surprises along the way; Frank revealed some old secrets that he hadn't told anyone before.

We talked at his kitchen table with a hand-held tape recorder running.

Characters and Places

FRANK: My grandfather.

PEACHES: My grandmother.

ANNE: Frank's wife in between his marriages to my grandmother. A very kind woman. She died several years ago.

ALEX: Frank and Anne's son. My uncle.

HILLCREST: The juvenile rehabilitation center where Frank finally got a job. (One that he didn't walk out on.)

November 3, 2004

FRANK: Is this going to be published in one of those little somnambulism books?

ME: Yeah.

F: It is, huh?

M: Yeah, so just tell me whatever you feel comfortable being published.

F: Okay.

PEACHES: I think you first oughtta tell her the story of the newspaper. The one you got from the newspaper.

F: I'll get to that.

M: So what was the first job you ever had?

F: Oh, the first job I ever had? Now you're throwing me off. The first job I ever had? It was picking raspberries. In Portland, in Southeast over by Market Street—about 101st and Market. I went to pick raspberries 'cause I wanted a bicycle and my parents wouldn't buy me a bicycle. So I went to work to earn it. I think it cost $27. But I don't recall if I earned the whole $27. I think they kicked in some. That was my first job. Did I quit that job? Well, with raspberry-picking jobs it's almost like you quit every day.

M: Why's that?

F: 'Cause you get paid every day. So I don't think I finished out the whole season. I went until I was able to get the bicycle.

M: Let's move on to the topic of jobs you walked out on.

F: Okay—these are just walked-off-the-job jobs. I don't have them in chronological order. The one I told you about—the choker setter job? I went to the Allegheny woods just outside of Coos Bay. I got a little shack. I was very enthusiastic. I was going to go "work in the woods." The little shack had an oil heater that I used to burn wood in, and I'm surprised that I just didn't burn the whole house down. Once I got the job I had to go to Weyerhauser, the company, and get in the truck. Then they'd drive us out to the job. And it seemed like it took hours but it probably didn't. And I was going to be a choker setter. Big muscles, you know?

And so I arrived on the job and the lumber man, the boss said, "Take this pulley (which was 50, 60 pounds) down that canyon and up the other side to that donkey."

The donkey was some sort of equipment they used. Maybe it had once been a real donkey. It pulled the logs up and down.

I made it down the hill. I started up the hill and I said, "Uh uh. This is not for me." Just left the donkey there and walked off. Left the hook and everything. Left it on the ground. I couldn't carry it anywhere, you know! I went up to the top. I didn't tell anyone anything. I saw the old dirt road and some guy stopped and gave me a ride. He was a Weyerhauser worker himself, I think. And so I quit. No words, nothing. I was a coward, probably. I didn't want to go face him. Or I was embarrassed that I quit and couldn't carry the thing. Was I disgusted with myself? No, I don't think so. But I did want to have a job. Everyone was always telling me, "Get a job, get a job." So I got a few jobs. But I just couldn't ... you know. Well with that one there ...

M: How old were you with that one?

F: I was an old quitter on that one. Like I was probably ...

M: What was your next one?

F: Well this is not the next one—it's one of. Well, myself and Major, my teenage friend, we wanted jobs. And knew about picking potatoes. The potato harvest was up in Redmond, Oregon. And it was that time of year. So we got all pumped about going up there. But we did not want to pick potatoes, we wanted to—

P: Buck 'em.

F: Buck 'em. Pick the sacks up off the ground after the picker picked 'em and put 'em on the truck. We got a shack. There was a shack on the property. And we filled it up with groceries and stuff. We were "there for the harvest" and we went to work. And it was hard, heavy work. I could barely lift them up on the truck. So one day—we got out of there, we quit. We didn't tell anybody. I think I just slinked off in the dark of the night.

M: Did you get paid every day?

F: I wasn't there long enough to find out. I never did get paid. I just disappeared. So I got one day's labor. See, I wanted to drive the truck. We both wanted to drive the truck. And we might've eventually both got to drive the truck. But we didn't, you know?

M: What happened to Major?

F: He went with me.

M: Did you have a conversation, you know, "let's quit this job?"

F: Yeah, and I don't know who was the one who instigated it. But I suspect it might've been me. We might've just been tired out and we had this notion of what the job was going to be like and it wasn't like that. Besides, we were young and we had other stuff to do. Like drink Tokay wine.

M: What's Tokay wine?

F: It's like 69 cents a—

P: Fortified wine.

F: I don't know. This was before fortified wine.

P: I don't know. M & F was fortified—

F: Oh, was it? Well anyway, I guess it was 59 cents a quart of wine. Tokay. So—that's what we did.

Okay. So here's one about "The Guy."

P: This is my favorite story.

F: Is it? Well, I answered an ad in the paper for a young person to come out and be a helper on a farmy kinda place. And you know, whatever, mow the lawn, or do dishes and that kind of stuff. So I was interviewed amongst a slug of other young people and he gave me the job. So that was cool. They gave me a room with a closet full of the latest, cool clothes.

P: Stratoveri shirts.

F: Stratoveri shirts. They were cool then, you know?

P: They were like $20 apiece. Which would be $150 now.

M: So these were nice clothes?

F: Yeah, a whole thing full of them.

M: Was it a family that had hired you?

F: Yeah. And he said I could use his car, a new Oldsmobile. Well, that's what really got me. That's what I focused on. During that day I was talking to his wife and his wife said, "Well (whatever his name was—Joe?), well Joe wants a boy who will take showers with him." So, you know, it kinda didn't dawn on me. I just said, "Okay."

So that evening when I was out driving the car it dawned on me what was happening. I was pretty naïve, I guess. So when I was done driving the car for the evening I just parked it somewhere and I quit that job.

M: So you don't remember whether you drove it back to his house or left it somewhere?

F: I don't remember.

M: Did you even spend the night there?

F: It was just that one day. So it just occurred to me—he had this whole closet full of all these nice clothes. He must've had some young boy living there before. Who ran off, too. He probably had to clothe them well to keep them there. So that was "The Guy." You got that?

P: Isn't that a bizarre story?

F: I worked out here in Troutdale. Like out in the field. Trimming plants, doing nursery work. I worked on that job a few days maybe. I don't know. I asked for the day off, 'cause I was gonna get married to Peaches and the guy wouldn't give me the time off so I just quit. Never went back. I had to get married, you know! That was about it. I don't think I ever got paid. She says she never remembers me getting any money.

P: Can I?

F: Yeah, go ahead.

P: The funny thing ... my dad got him that job. He'd get up in the morning, ride with my mom and dad. My mom and dad would drop him, go to their jobs, come back, pick him up. He did that for I don't know how long before my dad found out he had lost his job.

M: So what did you do—you'd get dropped off and then what would you do?

F: I don't remember that part.

P: Leave it to the wife to remember.

F: I probably just went off and went fishing. I used to go fishing a lot in those days. I really don't know what I did. I really don't have any recollection. She's a good recollector.

I got a job in Eastern Oregon. In the pea harvest. Major and I again.

P: Milton-Freewater.

F: Milton-Freewater.

M: The only hyphenated town in the US. Did you know that?

F: No, I didn't. We got this notion that we could go up there and get a job. We wanted to be truck drivers so bad. So we went up there "to be truck drivers." 'Cause we knew they needed people to drive trucks during the crops coming in. So we must've been old enough to have drivers' licenses. I know Major was. We went up there and were very enthusiastic about working. We wanted to make money. I think I drove my car on that one but I'm not sure. I had an old '41 Chevy. Anyway, I got the job. But they didn't give us the job driving any trucks. The closest we got to a truck was emptying a truck, which is what we did. The first four hours of the day we emptied the truck. The second four hours, we were gone. We quit. We quit right there. I quit ... it's so crazy, you know, looking back at it.

I got money for that job, One day in the future a letter came and I got a check for the four hours. That was nice.

I drove my old Chevy up there. I remember driving back. It had no lights. So I had to follow a truck. I followed this truck, in the rain, at night. As much as I could—or the next truck. All the way until I got to The Dalles or Hood River, and I was begging a guy to give me gas. I remember not having any money. And I remember him saying, "Oh, I can fix your lights." And he got a wire and hooked it straight onto the battery. But we quit that job after four hours.

M: Whatever happened to Major? Were you friends for a long time?

F: Major turned out okay. We were friends for quite a while. We probably still would be if we ever saw each other again. Major was called Major because his dad was a major in the army. Major went on to go to school. Last I saw him, he was going to school and learning to be a nurses' aide or something like that. I wouldn't have saw him then, but I found out he was doing that and it was when I first started using drugs. I went over to him to get a syringe.

M: Oh. Really?

F: He gave me this great big syringe.

M: He knew you were doing that and he gave you a syringe?

F: I don't know if he knew that or not. Anyway, he gave me a syringe. Which I never used. I think it was just at the beginning stages of using injectable drugs. I didn't know anything about it. No one ever used a syringe that big for drugs.

M: Was it like a horse syringe?

F: Actually, maybe they did. Like later on I was around people who used turkey basters for syringes.

M: How did they do that? They put a needle on the end of it?

F: They put a needle on the end of it. They'd fill it up with this stuff. I mean, they were hardcore. And they'd fill it up with ... they call it crank now? What is that stuff that is so popular? Methamphetamine?

M: Did they have methamphetamine back then?

F: What is the one that everyone is using now? We're always hearing about it.

P: Crack?

F: No, they call it meth? Well, in those days it was illegal to get methadrine. You could go in and get it at the drug store if they'd sell it to you. Some would, some wouldn't. And some people got so they used so much of it that none of the syringes would hold enough. So they'd put it in these turkey basters. With the big bulb on the end of it ... where were we?

I answered a classified ad. They wanted a salesman to sell for people to have their picture taken. I answered the ad. I thought I was going to make a lot of money.

One day. One day. *(He holds up his finger.)*

'Cause I talked to a couple of people and realized it was not the way I thought it was going to be. They gave me cards that had people's names on 'em that they got somewhere. So I was to go see these people. Since I had their name and they had showed some interest, I thought it was going to be a snap. *(He snaps.)* And it wasn't. It's just another example of me in those days. Just one day—took off. Didn't say anything to 'em. This is getting boring, 'cause you—

M: No. No it's not.

F: Well, you know—all these failures!

M: It's interesting that they would hire you. Maybe the culture is different now, but to be able to get all these jobs! You know what I mean? Did you give them a resume? Or did you just show up and they would hire you?

F: Yeah, nobody, I don't think anybody, ever—well, how could I have a resume? I was just a little kid!

Okay, this is a job I kept for a while but ended up walking out on. I sold encyclopedias. Collier's Encyclopedias. I was one among 50 people that went in to get the job. The rest of them disappeared 'cause they didn't want anything to do with it. It ended up me and four or five out of 50 who went to work. I sold encyclopedias door to door for maybe a year or more. And I did really well at it. I was good at it. I made a lot of money. I was even one of the top salesmen in ... the whole United States! I think. Wow.

M: Really?

F: Yeah.

M: Why were you good at it? What made you a good salesman?

F: I had a good, positive attitude. I'd knock on doors and talk to anybody. I didn't have any fear. And for those first three weeks I thought I was giving them away. They teach you this pitch that you're giving them away. I believed it. Until someone said to me, "We're not giving those away!"

M: What was the catch?

F: What it was, was you would knock on the door and they would answer the door. And you would tell them that you were wanting to place encyclopedias in their house as advertising. And that "we believed that word-of-mouth advertising was stronger than any other form of advertising. So would they accept this set of encyclopedias free for the advertising?" I mean, they said yes a lot, and that's why I made a lot of money.

M: But then what would happen? They'd get a bill in the mail?

F: Well, what it was ... we'd say, "Since you're gonna have these for advertising purposes we want you to keep it up to date." So every year they got a yearbook. Depending on what kind of set they had. If you thought they had a little more money you'd give them a yearbook that cost $29.95. We wanted them to keep them up to date for ten years. Which means that would cost them 299 odd bucks. Or we only wanted them, if they were poor, to keep them up to date for ten years for $19.95 a year.

So I did that for quite a while until I ran into this crew of people who were just so negative. They were older, they had been sales-men, they were burned out. They would tell my boss who would drive us around, "Oh, that's terrible territory there." They'd just look at the houses and know that nobody was gonna buy anything. And I just got really negative.

M: So then you quit?

F: I moved to San Francisco. And I just worked enough to barely survive in San Francisco, and then I just never—you know—never went back. Never went back.

Part of the enjoyment was that I thought it was pretty cool that I could say stuff to people and it would go right over their heads.

M: What would you have done if they heard you and they got really offended?

F: Well, that never happened.

One lady one time, she was questioning why I had knocked on her door. And I told her that I was involved in the delivery of the Superman comic books she had ordered.

We all got thrown in jail that night. Well, not thrown in jail. But we got taken into the police station. There was only four of us. They rounded us up.

M: Where were you?

F: They told us we were violating the "Green River Ordinance." It was ...

P: No salesmen.

F: No salesmen allowed.

P: No door-to-door salesmen.

F: The local businesses didn't like the salesmen coming in and taking the money out.

M: That was in Washington?

F: No, that was in Montana. So anyway, I walked away from that job.

M: Even though you had it for over a year.

F: Right. You know, I mean, that was ... I just.

I'm trying to think of other words to say what I did but that's basically what I did. I just never went back. Okay?

Okay—here's a job: I was a pin setter in a bowling alley. Along with all the homeless and the hobos and bums of the world. They worked there, too. It was a job you could go in, work one day. Then they would go get on a train. They'd disappear. So I worked there. Then I just disappeared.

M: Now explain that to me because I can't think of a time when I haven't seen the automatic machines. How does that work?

F: Well, we were in the back. It wasn't automatic. The thing that made it go down was this. It had this bar across there and you went "KRICK" like that. And then the pins would set up. So you would do it in this alley here and then you would do two alleys and if you were *really* good you could do three.

P: And you had to get your feet up 'cause when a bowling ball came down, you were liable to get whacked with one of those pins. So there was a place you got up above the pins, above the opening.

M: If you were bowling you could see the people back there doing it?

P: Yeah.

F: They could see our feet and they could see us reach down and get the pins. 'Cause they'd knock 'em down and they were in this pit. And we got to reach down in the pit and pick 'em up and throw 'em in that thing that goes down. And then "KRICK" like that. Nowadays they probably wouldn't let people do that, 'cause those pins are heavy and sometimes they'd go "WHEEE" *(over his head)*. We'd yell at the guys, "Not so fast!"

M: Did you ever associate with any of the guys you worked with?

F: No. They didn't show any enthusiasm about talking to me.

M: They just got their money ...

F: They just got their booze and moved on. Or their food or whatever. Some of 'em didn't drink, I guess.

Okay? So that was the kind of job I quit, but that was also the kind of job that people just worked one day. So probably most of the people that worked there were quitters.

M: Right.

F: Which is probably why they were there—because they were quitters.

Okay.

I went to a place in North Portland. There was a place that delivered eggs. They had a bunch of egg trucks and they delivered eggs, butter, cottage cheese, and that kind of stuff. And I went in and I asked the guy (a truck again was involved), I asked if I could get a job. He said, "No, all my routes are full." So I said, "Well what if I *get* a route?" (You see I had already sold encyclopedias so I was feeling good about that.) "What if I got enough customers for a route?"

And he said, "Well, yeah. Sure." In the back of his mind thinking, "Yeah this is *not* gonna happen."

So I did. I went out and I dressed like a farmer boy. I even put straw in my cuffs a couple times. (Just a couple times.) In those days you could go around and knock on people's doors and they wouldn't get mad or slam it or call the police. So that's what I did over in North Portland. I'd knock on the door and talk to the ladies. That's who they were: mostly ladies. They wanted somebody to deliver fresh eggs to them and cheese and chicken. I got enough customers that he got me started on a route. So I worked there for ... months. I don't know how many but ... months. And I don't know ... oh, that was in the days that I was experimenting with drugs. And at that time I think I was experimenting with tranquilizers. That was the thing back in those days. You'd hear about it in the news, people taking tranquilizers. Miltown, that was the big name. Equanil.

M: Those were the brand names?

F: Yeah.

M: And they were legal? You could just get them at a pharmacy?

F: It depends on the pharmacy. The laws weren't as strict then.

You could get them by prescription. You could get a prescription. In those days you could just call a doctor, and he'd say, "Okay. What drugstore do you want the prescription at?" And he'd call and get you a prescription. And you know, I'd take those things and I'd get awful sleepy. 'Cause they were tranquilizers—they made you tranquil. So that, and I don't know if I was smoking pot in those days or not. I had, but I don't know if I was at the point where it affected me keeping a job or not. It probably ... I don't know.

I quit.

Move on?

M: I have to go to the bathroom. Just a sec.

(A sec.)

F: This is the one ... well I have the tendency to minimize or maximize or interpret these things, the importance and so on ...

I was a cesspool digger, self-employed.

My buddy Major and I, we dug three cesspools. They were eighteen feet deep, you know. We had a winch and it had a rope on it. One guy would dig and the other would crank the winch and then we would trade off. So, depending on the type of soil, the guy that was digging could fill up a five-gallon bucket and just kinda kick back while the other guy was winding it up. So we did three cesspools. We were gonna be cesspool entrepreneurs.

P: They could make about $150 a cesspool, which was a lot of money in those days.

F: Yeah. So we had our own winch.

M: So I don't understand what exactly a cesspool is.

F: That's where the sewage went.

M: It's like a septic tank but there's no tank?

F: It "fed the earth." It was like a big hole in the ground. After you got it dug, they would have a guy who you really looked up to. He was a brick guy and he would line it with bricks. We just dug it.

I was telling Peaches we were lucky we didn't get killed. Because they'd cave in sometimes. But we only had one cave-in. We never did finish that. It was in the Rockwood area. The soil was so rocky and hard to work over there that we never finished that one. So anyway, it was just another example of getting enthusiastic about something and then quitting.

M: So you did three of them and then you quit?

F: Yeah. We tried to do one for a barber. There was a barber shop on 96th and Division. We wanted to dig his cesspool and we told him we'd dig it if he gave us free haircuts for the rest of our lives. But he wouldn't do that. He was an adult, you know, and I don't know what went through his mind. It would've been a good deal for him 'cause he could've died the next week and not have to give any haircuts. Or we might've moved away, or might've died in a cesspool.

At the Multnomah Athletic Club in Portland. It's got all the decks where people eat and watch the ball game. It's this posh club. I was basically a gopher, but they called me a page boy and I would go around and say, "Calling Dr. Smith!" But I didn't really like doing that much so I'd just go up and I'd say, "Who's Dr. Smith?"

I felt really awkward doing that. But I'd figure out some way to find the guy. They didn't have intercoms, you know. This was in the '50s.

M: Did you have to wear one of those little suits and carry a platter?

F: I did have a platter. A suit? I might have had a suit. I can't remember. That was another job where I competed with a multitude and got the job. I was good at getting jobs. I didn't get fired. I just quit. My guess is I gave notice on the job. That might've been the way I got paid. I do not know.

In Seattle, Washington. I got a job in a movie theater. Picking up all the stuff people left and the bathrooms and the carpet. I don't remember how long I had that job but I don't think it was more than one day. Maybe two. That was a bad move. That was one of the bad moves in my life because I was flat broke. No money, nowhere to live. I was in the early stages of using drugs. In those days we would ... druggies were drinking this cough syrup. That's why I went to Seattle, 'cause you could get it in Washington. It got so you couldn't get it in Oregon.

M: So you moved to Seattle 'cause you could get cough syrup there?

F: Yeah. In fact, my goal was to live in this old hotel that was right above a drugstore. But anyway, that was a bad move on my part.

My dad lived in Edmonds so a couple times while I was up there I got him to come and see me and give me $20. And he would give me $20 and he was out of there. Basically we didn't really talk about anything. I needed the money. But that was good of him. I liked that.

So I lived in an old hotel and was getting kicked out. You know they won't let you stay in those places. One of those old hotels, I think the rooms were a couple bucks a night.

M: I think they still have some of those old hotels in Portland. Is that the kind of place it was—a weekly hotel, daily hotel?

F: Probably more of a weekly hotel. You could live there if you had money. You didn't really cook in 'em. I suspect people probably did fix themselves food. They didn't have microwaves. They probably had cold food, bologna sandwiches.

So anyway, that was just another job. That was a bad mistake. I was in big trouble as far as eating and so on. I don't think I begged but I was close to, uh ...

M: Homelessness.

F: Yeah. I must've ... I don't know how I got out of that situation. I probably came back to Portland and my guess is I hitchhiked 'cause that was my method of transportation in those days. A lot. Lots of times.

M: What kind of cough syrup was it? What was in it?

F: Codeine and stuff called dihydrocodeine. It had chloroform in it, it had antihistamines. I'm not really sure what was in it that made people like it so much. But almost everyone I knew that went through that phase of drinking that cough syrup moved on to using heroin. They just did. You got so you couldn't get that stuff any more, anyway. You got deathly sick from it, too. Like when you first started taking it if you drank too much, you'd get deathly sick. I'd go in a restaurant with someone and I'd say, "Excuse me for a minute." And I'd go back to use the bathroom, and they'd tell me, "We could hear you clear back in the bathroom back there heaving!" I'd just get pale. It was horrible stuff. But it felt good. When you weren't sick, it was nice.

P: Is that in retrospect or was that at the time?

F: At the time it was nice when you weren't sick.

I sold ladies shoes at a Portland department store. It was called Olds and Kings. And it's now that block. It's a place now that's a block.

P: It's the place where they have those little shops inside.

M: The Galleria?

F: Yeah. That whole building was like Meier and Frank's. It was competition downtown. So I worked there in the ladies shoe department. A couple weeks maybe.

And ... I quit. I don't remember ... the reason I didn't stick around to get money was 'cause I wasn't sticking around. And they always have some sort of procedure, "Well, okay. We'll send it to you ... "

I just quit, I took off.

Here's a dishwasher job in the Morgan building in Portland. Downstairs in this building there was a pool hall. I washed dishes there and I also worked there in the evenings making deli sandwiches for my friends. They kept it open for some reason at night, but there was hardly ever any business. So I washed dishes there. The policeman on that beat was so pleased.

M: Why?

F: He'd come in every day and say, "Frank, you're working. I'm so happy to see you working."

M: He knew you?

F: Yeah, 'cause I was working in an area where I used to hang around the pool hall. My buddies, we'd hang around that part of town. We were the cool guys, you know. He was Pimples. We all called him Pimples. 'Cause his face had acne.

M: Did you call him that to his face?

F: No, no. Pimples was one of those guys who didn't give you a break. Some of 'em would, they'd look the other way. To just have you around—Pimples didn't like that. He didn't even want you in his area. Even if you weren't doing anything wrong, he didn't want you in his area. I've run into other people like that, too. There were some policemen that didn't want me in their—well, basically, Portland. So, it makes their job easier. If they can get the riffraff out.

P: You were so likeable! I don't understand that!

(He laughs.)

F: What do you mean?

(She laughs.)

F: Okay, that's dishwasher. I quit there. No great big dramatic stories. The whole bunch of them makes them dramatic. Each is just a chintzy little job.

I got a job in Salem. This was when I was in my middle 30s. I got the job. I was supposed to go the next day. Didn't even go.

M: You didn't work there? Really?

F: I signed all the papers and everything. I had the job but I never actually did it. I guess I quit 'cause I was hired. There was another cannery in West Salem. I worked there a few days in the green bean harvest. They had these conveyor belts that ran different places with green beans on 'em. My job was to sweep any green beans that fell off the conveyor belts and throw 'em away. They probably gave 'em to ...

P: Pig farmers.

F: I worked there two or three days. I think I had already graduated from college and I thought, "I'm not gonna be a cannery worker!"

M: You were a taxi driver?

F: I drove taxi for about twelve hours a day in Salem. It was close to the time I was going to school. You were busy the whole time. It might've been between terms. I wanted a job really badly. I think Anne and I were married and I think Alex might've been born. I wanted that job but they wouldn't give it to me. The company wouldn't give it to me. The company said (I told them I had been in jail, in prison), and they said, "Oh, the city ordinance won't let you do that, you can't work."

So I said to myself, "Uh huh."

So I had my case brought up before the city council, the council chambers in Salem, and they changed the law. I say changed the law ... they changed something. 'Cause they told the cab driver people, "Oh yeah, he can work." It was in the newspaper ... somebody told me they heard it on the radio, it was kind of a big deal. And so I drove maybe a couple weeks or so. It was not a fun job. It was a hard job.

M: In Salem, what kind of people would be in taxis?

F: Drunks ... and doctors' offices. That's a lot of cab business, taking people to doctors' offices. But I worked mostly at night, so a lot of drunks and a lot of poor people. That surprised me. I would've guessed that cabs were for rich people but they have their own cars and people to drive them around, I guess.

M: So when did you get your job at Hillcrest?

F: Oh. I got my job at Hillcrest ... I had graduated from college. (*He laughs.*)

F: It chokes me up.

(*He starts to cry. I turn off the tape.*)

F: I'm so emotional about this.

M: Why does it make you so emotional? Just to think about

all the stuff that you went through and how this was your saving grace?

F: Sure.

M: You're very lucky. Do you feel lucky?

F: Well I feel lucky, and I feel also like *I* did a big thing. After being in the slammer three times. *(He holds up his fingers.)*

M: Whoa. I didn't know that.

F: And so I never quit another job after that. I kept that job.

I went in and I talked to a lady. Margaret. She was a lady that cared about people. She liked me and she liked what I had done. She liked the comeback. Plus, Hillcrest dealt with crooks and people who didn't do well in life. So to meet one that did probably meant something to her. So she said, "I'm going to talk to some people about getting you a job."

M: And you had your psychology degree?

F: I'm sure that played a part. So she said she was gonna talk to some people to see if she could get me a job there. And she did. But they had to set up an interview for me and there had to be a job there that was open—but she fixed all that stuff. And I went into the interview and they gave me the job. No one else was gonna get that job 'cause she had already decided that ...

P: You were gonna have it.

F: *(He's choked up.)* So I started there on-call. And I just worked my way up. Stayed there, basically.

M: Did you know that you wanted to work with prisoners? Was that something you felt you had a calling for?

F: I did.

P: When we get through here I want you to tell her the things that you did when you were in prison—the jobs that you had?

F: Oh, you are just gonna get me going today, huh?

P: Well, you might as well.

F: Well this is supposed to be about ...

M: It can be about whatever.

F: Well? Where were we? Hillcrest? I got most every job at Hillcrest by interviewing. Being one amongst many. But I'm a pretty good interviewer. Even when I didn't interview well, I'd get a job. I'd walk out and think, "Who would hire me?" And sure enough ... *(He's rifling through some papers.)*

There's a form here that tells a lot about my work record. My general work record. My work history. I can't find it. What it is is a form that lists all the jobs that you've had—that you've reported. But it shows all these jobs I've had over this period of time and then there is this big space where I never worked all these years. No jobs. And then when I went to work at Hillcrest it all started.

What was it that you wanted me to tell her?

P: The jobs you had when you were in prison. I think that was very interesting.

F: You do, huh?

I was a schoolteacher. I taught spelling.

M: Oh really? To other prisoners?

F: Everywhere you go they have money problems. In the prison they had a school. A lot of people had never been to school, didn't go to grade school or anything. So I taught spelling to all these prisoners. In the day I'd teach, I'd just have a few in my class. But at night I'd teach 'cause they all wanted to get out of their cells. Talk to people. My classes would be full at night. They were always respectful. They'd talk and I'd be up there writing words out. The ones that wanted to learn, they'd learn. I taught one guy ... how to read.

M: From scratch? He didn't know anything?

F: That was great. I really liked that because it just changed his life. I suppose he really liked me for doing that. He was from the south. I just got a bunch of old books they had around the school. And taught him the alphabet, and the sounds—diphthongs and all of that.

M: Did you get paid for that?

F: Not at first. I eventually got paid like 25 cents a day.

M: So basically you didn't get paid.

F: No, but when I got a quarter a day, that, plus me giving blood was enough to buy cigarettes.

M: Oh my gosh.

F: Well, giving blood was easy. We gave blood for some kind of hepatitis. Some kind of coughing thing. Some research thing. Like every ten weeks you could give a jug of blood. They'd pay you maybe $10. That's pretty good money.

M: Are you ever amazed that you didn't get any diseases from using needles? Did you use needles?

F: Oh yeah.

P: You oughtta see the scars on his arms.

F: I have this picture in my mind of being in this old, dirty old hotel off of First or Second on the west side. I don't even know if it's there any more. The room was about as big as a couple bathrooms. Somebody lived there. They had a bed and a sink and probably a chair. And there was sitting on the table this glass. And the water was yellow in it. And we were all using that water. We would put our stuff in there and then we would clean our needles out. It's just horrifying to me now that I could ever do anything like that. There would be blood in there. We'd use that water for mixing our drugs ... so what was the question?

M: You are amazed.

F: Oh yeah.

P: You forgot to tell her the rest of your jobs in prison.

F: Well, the first couple of years I worked in the school, plus I was doing my own school stuff. Getting my GED. The second time I was there I got a job in a dental lab and I taught school at night. I made false teeth.

M: Out of what? Porcelain?

F: And plastic. Some people liked porcelain, some of them liked plastic. The people that didn't like porcelain would usually say, "I don't want that clacking sound." But yeah, it was a professional teeth-making place. The doctor would make the impression and we would make a model and we would make a thing like a person's mouth. And we had a model of their gums and then we would set the little teeth on it. And so I did that for a fair amount of time for that second sentence. I don't know if that was the second ... I don't think I worked there the last time ... I think I was involved in school. I got involved in an experimental program through the federal government. It was called Upward Bound. There was 25 or 30 people in the prison that got interviewed and got selected for it—so I did, too. "Mr. Interview Man." And I went to school. Took college classes.

M: Did you ever get your high school diploma?

F: Just my GED.

P: The first time you were in.

F: No, the first time I was in I taught school. The first time I was in, the only thing I thought about was getting out and getting drugs. That was it. Whenever I would talk to anyone about getting out, I would talk about getting out and getting drugs. Which is just what I did.

M: How long were you out before you got back in again?

F: A year.

P: Most of the 1960s you were in prison ...

F: Yeah.

P: Seven years all together wasn't it?

F: Yeah. I worked at a farm outside of Salem. I worked at this farm for a while.

P: Did you quit that job?

F: No. No, I didn't. I was working there as a janitor inside the building. The lieutenant there liked my work so well that he recommended me to go to this forest camp down at Tillamook. I'm laughing about the reason why he liked me 'cause it was on the second floor of this big building where the people slept. I kept all the beds all even—you could put a string down it. And I kept it real neat and he really liked that and so he sent me on to a camp where I planted trees.

M: And this is still while you were in prison?

F: Like the last few months before I left. That was the second time I was there. The third time I was there, when I left early it was 'cause I went to college. It was a weird group. All us guys that got out of prison went to U of O.

M: Did you ever look around at the students and think, "If you only knew?"

F: Oh, I think they knew. 'Cause we would sit around in the SU. And that's where we would congregate. And some of them would end up with girlfriends. And pretty much people knew. But I don't think we were up to keeping it a secret. In fact it was kind of a badge of honor. Being an ex-convict and being out there and going to school and making something out of yourself—you know there was a certain pride in it.

What was it I was supposed to tell her?

P: About all the jobs you had in prison ... the thing that amazes me is that you got out and he still was going to college to finish up and you had to put yourself through the last year.

F: Right—they paid for my schooling the first three months I was out and the next three months they paid for less and the final three months they paid for less and that was it. So, of course Anne was working and then I got money from the GI Bill so we did okay. And part of the time—well, Anne had been in jail.

P: Prison or jail?

F: Prison. She was next to the men's prison in a women's prison. So she went down to the federal government and they had these programs and she qualified really fast for one program 'cause she had been in prison. She was a dope fiend and what else? She was a woman. They had these criteria, you know. And the worse you were, the better you qualified. So she qualified for completely free rent—I mean nothing. She didn't have to pay any rent for a while.

A year or so. So with that, and my GI Bill, and she was working part of the time until Alex was born ...

P: When did you get on the methadone program?

F: Me?

P: Both of you.

F: She was one of the first people ever on the methadone program in Oregon. She must've got on in the early '60s. In fact, most of her family was on the methadone program.

M: Oh really?

F: Well, not her mom and dad.

M: But her siblings ...

F: She had several brothers and a couple sisters.

M: She had a big family, didn't she?

P: Wasn't it eleven?

F: Yeah. And most of 'em were on the methadone program. One of 'em was a drunk. There might have been one of them that wasn't any of that stuff. They were all devout Christians.

M: They must have gone through some hard times. Obviously if the whole family ... if they all got into drugs. That's crazy.

F: Yeah. Mom and Dad were devout Christians and they never got into any trouble.

M: Why do you think all of them got into so much trouble?

F: It seems like it all started when they lived in San Francisco. They lived over in the Mission District and her mom always told me that from that point on, things just fell apart.

P: They went downhill.

F: Yeah. But she was on the program probably longer than any other human being. Especially in Oregon, maybe in the United States.

P: So you got on it after you were in prison?

F: Yeah, I got on it when I was getting out of prison because I was afraid.

P: You were afraid you'd go back to it so you got on it.

F: Yeah, I was afraid. I was on it when I was going to college. I remember one day they called me from the clinic while I was at college. They had given me the wrong dosage at the methadone clinic. I guess they figured I was gonna die or something. *(He laughs.)* I didn't ... they must have got it all mixed up somehow—thought they'd given me the wrong dosage. I didn't notice. But I got off the methadone program because—I got the job at Hillcrest and I was still on the methadone program. And I was on call so I'd work all kind of hours, the graveyard shift, the day shift. In those days you had to get your methadone by some certain time, by 8:00 or something in the morning. If you had a job and couldn't make it, that didn't make any difference to them. Those were the rules and you had to do that. I just ...

P: Well, it was a good incentive.

F: It was?

P: To get off.

F: It turned out it was for me. But I don't know that it was ...

M: It was maybe a good incentive to start using heroin again for some people, right? I mean, they would go crazy and want to get it and they couldn't get the methadone so they would go out and get some heroin. Is that what would happen?

F: That's probably what would happen. Or some people would get their methadone and they'd save a little bit every day and then sell it. But then they got so you'd have to drink it in the clinic. But some people would keep some in their mouths and go outside and spit it in a glass or something and give it to their friends.

M: Oh God!

F: I know!

P: Think how sick they would be of themselves if they were off of it and thought about that.

F: When they told me that I would have to go pick it up, I did that for a very short amount of time. Maybe a few days—I just got that job at Hillcrest. I was already going down on my dosage.

Because I had decided that, uh ... something earlier that had happened at the methadone clinic had made me decide to get off the program. And I was down to a couple milligrams a day. Most people were taking 35.80. In those days they would give them these big doses. I got down to the point that when this happened, I could just say, "Adios, I'm never coming back again!"

M: Was it still really hard, though?

F: No.

M: It wasn't?

F: I was done and I was working, and I didn't have any problem at all. Now if I had been taking a big dose I would have had a problem. But I was tired of dealing with those people at the methadone program. They had all these rules and I understand now why they did, because it would be chaos there if they didn't. And I just decided that I just wanted to be a person and to be responsible for myself and not have to go run to mommy-methadone clinic, making all my decisions for me. So I got off it and that was the end of it.

P: So how did Anne get her methadone when she was dying?

F: Well, they changed the methadone program since the time I got off. She was on a lot of years after I got off. She was on the whole 30 years we were together.

M: Did she ever seriously try to get off it?

F: One time she got off it 'cause she thought it was making her cough. She lasted about eight months but she got back on because whatever—I don't recall. Her being off caused something healthwise. So she got back on.

M: I have to go to the bathroom. I'll be right back.

(I'm back.)

F: You know, one of the reasons I had success after all this stuff that went on in my life is 'cause I cut off all my old friends, everybody that used drugs, all the people that I knew in those days. I never would talk to them again. I never looked 'em up. If I saw them I'd look the other way. 'Cause I was afraid they would still be using drugs and I didn't want to have anything to do with that, okay? And all these years when Anne was on the methadone program and she would run into these people at the clinic and they'd say, "How is Frank doing?" and I'd never call. I just wouldn't do it. To this day, I don't have anything to do with those kind of people. So—what I'm leading to, is—I don't know what you're gonna do with this stuff but I don't mind my first name being used but I don't want my last name being used. Because I don't want one of them reading it and calling me up ...

M: Right. I'll write out what I'm gonna write and I'll have you look at it and you can approve it or have me change it.

F: Okay. Right. Because I don't trust 'em. I know what they're like 'cause I was the same way. So it's easy for me to not trust 'em. And I don't want to have anything to do with them ... that's something I'm not proud of—not giving people the benefit of the doubt.

P: Well you do—but when it comes to drugs or seamy behavior you don't.

M: 'Cause you understand the mentality.

F: Right.

P: Did you want to go into how you supported your drugs?

F: Well, she probably has to go to school or something.

M: *(I laugh.)* Well if you don't want to talk about it that's fine. I don't have to be anywhere until work.

F: Oh, I could talk about it.

M: This is when you weren't working? This is when you got really heavy into drugs?

F: This is when I, uh ...

P: This is why he went to prison.

F: This started off the drug thing. It started off with ... well, I smoked a little pot. But it really wasn't a big factor in my life. Using the cough syrup was the big factor. Speed—we called it speed in those days. When I got to the point where I needed money, the cough syrup was only a buck or so. So you could somehow scrounge up a buck or so. It didn't require you to go out and commit crimes. But when I started using heroin then I had to steal to get money.

So I saw this guy one time down at the pool hall. Murphy? Was it Murphy? I don't remember. But anyway, he came in and opened up his coat and he was showing this guy like a new camera or a coffee pot—something new. I think it might have been a camera ... and there was a camera store right above. The pool hall was downstairs but on the street level there was a camera shop. It might still be around town. He was trying to sell this thing. It was worth quite a bit of money. So I got involved in the conversation and discovered that he had stole it. Upstairs. He went in and just stuck it under his coat and walked out. And he said that he would get paid a third of its value. And the light goes on for me—I thought, "I could do that."

That's what I started doing. I had an old coat. A little topcoat and I would go around to these different stores and stick things underneath it. Like if I wanted that, I would just take it and stick it under my coat.

M: Who would you sell it to?

F: The longer I did it, the more people there were to buy things.

M: These people had money to spend on things?

F: Oh yeah. Surprisingly, a large amount of the things I sold were to people who owned stores themselves.

M: Oh really? They didn't know you had stolen it?

F: Oh yeah, they knew.

M: Why didn't they turn you in?

F: Because I sold them stuff for a third—

M: You wouldn't steal from the same store and then sell it back to them?

F: Well I would've done that, but I normally didn't do that, though, because it was nice to have somebody to sell your stuff to so you wanted to keep your relations going ... *(He laughs.)*

M: So you would steal from one store and sell to another store.

F: Right.

M: And they knew it was stolen?

F: Yeah they knew. It wasn't a secret. They wanted stolen stuff. They could get it for a third and sell it for ...

P: For full price.

M: Even though they were encouraging people to steal and people were stealing from them as well?

F: Well everybody was stealing from everybody!

M: That's bizarre.

F: There were businesses all around Portland that I sold stuff to.

P: Drug stores?

F: Yeah, there was a guy that owned a drugstore up on 23rd Street up there. He would give me drugs for TVs and things. Or he would sell me drugs for money. But a lot of it was just merchandise trades.

P: Frank went to prison 'cause he got caught stealing a TV out of Smith's Home Furnishings. Which is down on Division Street where the Nature's is.

M: Division Street? Oh, that Wild Oats up there?

F: Yeah, but that was later on.

M: Did the guy that ran the drugstore, did he ever go to prison? Did any of these business owners ever go to prison?

F: No ... *I* ended up going to prison. And he just kind of ... his life went on and he no longer had the drugstore. I don't know what happened to him. He probably has a pharmacy somewhere. He never got arrested.

So anyway, I learned how to take these things. And hey—I was making a lot of money then. They were selling drugs around. Heroin. So I'd just go out and steal stuff and go buy heroin. And then steal more and go buy heroin. And pretty soon in town I pretty much burned my bridges. So I got a car, expanded my area and took up with a friend who also used heroin. We'd get up in the morning just like we had a job and we'd go out and drive around. I call it now "opportunity theft." We'd just go out and drive until an opportunity presented itself.

P: This is low carb.

(She hands me some toast.)

M: Looks good.

P: This is to hold you over until lunch.

F: So we'd just drive around. We'd drive around to TV stores and appliance stores. We'd drive around the back. More times than not the door would be open. There'd be a big door and nobody would be back there and there wasn't cameras in those days.

M: Oh yeah.

F: So we'd just go back and pick up a TV or two or whatever it is we wanted and we'd put it in the car. And we'd drive over to one of our—we called them "fences" and we'd sell the stuff for a third.

M: What's a fence?

F: A guy who deals in stolen property. And we would get the money from him and then we'd drive directly to the dope dealer and we'd spend the money on dope. We'd save enough money for gas for the next day and to eat on. That's about it.

M: Where'd you live at that time?

F: We'd live in different places. Hotels.

M: You didn't have any stuff? You had nothing.

F: No, not much.

P: Minnie died in 1960 and Andy died in '62.

M: These are your friends?

F: My adopted Mom and Dad.

M: Oh.

F: So that's how I earned the money.

P: But my point is that he could count on going there in a pinch.

M: Right. You knew you had that to fall back on.

F: Well it would have to *really* be a pinch. When Minnie was alive I could do it more, but when she died ...

Back to how we earned the money ... it was pretty much the same way the whole time. It got to be so we couldn't drive around Portland.

M: People knew you?

F: We'd taken everything that anybody was going to ... I mean, we'd go back to the same place. We'd go back and back—pretty soon we knew we shouldn't go back any more.

M: Warehouses and stuff?

F: Yeah, warehouses. Like we'd take cartons of cigarettes out of the back end of Safeway and other stores. They didn't lock it up. You'd just go in the back door and if they said, "What are you doing back here?"—*if* they did, you'd say, "I'm looking for these boxes." And they'd say, "Okay," and we'd go and take these cases of cigarettes—those were our big money-makers.

M: Where would you sell them?

F: To these people that I was telling you about. Mom and Pop stores. They'd sell 'em. So we had to keep expanding. I got so I'd drive to Gresham and to Beaverton. McMinnville. I'd go down to Medford or Tacoma. Lots of driving.

M: What kind of car was it?

F: I had lots of different cars. My most productive one was one of the early vans—'cause we could get a lot of stuff in the van.

So, that was the stealing part.

M: So it was just a matter of time before you got caught, you were doing so much of it?

F: Yeah. Right.

M: Did you think about that at the time, that you knew you were gonna get caught eventually?

F: Yeah. I think so.

M: But you didn't care.

F: No, I didn't. Well ... I didn't want to go to prison! But I didn't care enough to stop.

M: Right, and how could you? Did you ever go into rehab? Did they even have a place like that?

F: They may have, but I was never involved in any. Now and then I would say this is it, this is enough, and I would get some—it's called a dolophine—and it was like methadone. But the dolophine is in pill form. I'd get a bunch of those and go out of town somewhere and I'd say, "Okay, I'm gonna clean up now and I'm not gonna steal and I'm not gonna do anything." Then I'd stay there until the dolophine was all gone. Then I'd come back ...

P: And be all fresh for some more ...

F: Yeah, all ready. Yeah ... that's about it.

P: So prison was a good thing.

M: Could you get drugs in prison?

F: The last time I was there, there was a fair amount of pot. Not a fair amount—there was pot there. The first two times I was there, I never ran across any. The last time I was there they had changed the visiting situation where a person could have physical contact with their visitors. Like they could kiss—husband and wife. So the wife would have a little packet in her mouth and she'd give it to the guy and he would swallow it. He would get it out—however they do that stuff. I think there are a lot more drugs now. I hear about it on TV.

The last time I was there, there was pot. And not a lot of pot. I just knew this guy whose attorney would bring him pot. And that was the only guy I knew. There might have been others. It was different then. Because the population of the whole prison was not over a thousand people. Now I don't know what it is. They could watch everyone then. Everywhere you went you had to walk in a line. They watched everything you did. So it was hard for anyone to do anything.

M: Do you feel like having a job that you care about helped you a lot, or do you think that you learned to care about yourself more? When you got your job at Hillcrest ...

F: Well, it was myself and family. Me, and family, *and then* the job was an important means to that. The job was an important means to changing my thinking around, too. I couldn't work in a place with all that crummy thinking that I had in the past. So I was surrounded by people—staff that were involved in rehabilitation and getting things right. So that affected my thinking a lot, too. So it had a big impact on me. I would ... well, it just had a huge impact on me.

M: Do you feel like there is a certain amount of hopelessness that went along with your previous lifestyle and the jobs and the people that you met? As far as ... well, were they thinking about the future?

F: Who's they?

M: Oh, like people you were working with at the bowling alley or something ... they were just living day to day?

F: Well, maybe. But in those days when I was doing those things I wasn't thinking about that stuff. I never thought about hopelessness or ... hope.

M: Right. But in retrospect?

F: In retrospect they were living day to day, on the road. You could call it a life of hopelessness. They might have had hope but didn't know how to put it together. They had drinking problems. A lot of them were drunks.

M: You never became a drunk, though. It was more just drugs?

F: No. I drank some beer for a while and some wine for a while. But not very much. When I was in the army I drank a little whiskey. But I didn't know how to handle it. I was the kind of drunk who would run out in front of a pickup truck. I was not a good drunk.

M: You got too out of control.

F: Yeah I did. I got *way* out of control. Well, I didn't know how to drink. I didn't drink one drink or two.

M: You would just get hammered.

F: Yeah, I would. And it would be fast, too. If I had a container yay full—that meant to me: empty it. And that's pretty much the way I drank. I could buy whiskey in Kansas. They had these giant bottles of Old Crow—you could buy like a gallon or two.

P: It's a wonder you didn't kill yourself drinking.

F: It is, 'cause I didn't know how to drink. I even drank a bootleg whiskey one time. A guy was selling it when I was in the army. He was selling it out of the back of his car.

M: Like moonshine?

F: I think that's what it was, 'cause the seal was broken on it. He probably made it or watered it down or added something to it. I never did that again.

M: So did you have anything else you would like to have in this story ... about work or anything?

F: Work? No, that was our goal ... about quitting jobs. I could tell you how I felt about it but, uh ...

M: How did you feel about it?

F: When I did it?

M: Yeah.

F: I didn't. I didn't. I just quit and life just went on.

M: Did you ever feel like you were gaining experience in a variety of different trades, like you were becoming a renaissance man?

F: No, no, no.

M: You never gave a second thought to ...

F: No, no, no.

P: I think Frank was a runner. He'd always been a runner. Until he got Hillcrest under his belt.

F: Yeah. You mean when things weren't going right I'd move on?

M: That's the way you solved your problems.

F: Yeah, I often do that.

P: When he was a kid when he went to live with Minnie and Andy, he ran away I don't know how many times.

F: Yeah I did. I'd just run away and I'd go out and hitchhike.

Sometimes a car was coming one way I'd hitchhike, and then one coming the other way ... it didn't matter to me.

P: Often times he would go to Minnie's brother or sister instead of strangers. He was really a young kid.

F: I think I was thirteen the first time I ran away. By the time I got there they would call.

M: Were you punished?

F: No.

M: What would they say to you?

F: Well, "Glad to have you back."

M: How would you feel?

F: I don't think I felt much in those days. I can't recall. I didn't get spanked, I didn't get grounded. I might get a little bit of conversation about the consequences of what might happen to me when I was doing that. But I don't even know that. I just don't remember.

M: Did you feel like they didn't give you any boundaries?

F: No, I had boundaries. I couldn't do whatever I wanted. Andy, he was from the old country—he was raised in Spain, you know. So he had a lot of the old country ways. One of them was being in at a certain time of night. I spent many nights sleeping in the car 'cause they wouldn't let me in.

M: Oh really?

F: I had a time when I was supposed to be in, and they—

P: They'd lock the door.

F: They told me don't come home if you're not here, so I'd sleep in the car.

M: That's harsh!

F: Huh?

M: That's harsh.

F: It did get cold in the car.

P: But it didn't bring you in earlier.

F: No, it didn't bring me in earlier.

Childhood and Other Near-Death Experiences

FROM AGES SIX to eighteen I lived with my parents and six siblings in a mobile home on the side of a mountain in Corbett, Oregon. The road leading out of our property was roughly three miles long and dropped 500 feet down switchbacks and blind corners till it collided with the first real instruction: the stop sign at the bottom of the hill. By the time I got my driver's license, every inch of Loudon Road had already been imprinted onto my bones and muscles; every stomach-flipping turn, every brake and acceleration, every way to cheat death in order to save myself half-a-second of travel time had been stored up in the tissues of my body. My parents taught me this: how to drive "country," how to drive like a crazy person, how to survive my own death wish. And to top it off, in all the time leading up to my twelfth year, us kids were never required to wear our seatbelts.

The turning point came when we flipped my dad's Hyundai one morning in 1992 on our way to school. I was in the front seat. Dad was driving. And my sisters Sarah, Ana, and Zoe were in the backseat. None of us were strapped in. It was a crisp, cold morning at the end of November and we were listening to the oldies radio station. As usual, Dad had a cup of coffee in one hand and the other hand on the wheel. We hit some frost at 25 miles an hour and he lost control of the car. We went up on a little bank and the

Hyundai turned over as neatly as an over-easy egg. Lucky for the tender yolks inside, we didn't break. It all happened so fast that I opened my eyes, spread out my fingers, and found myself crumpled up in a ball on the roof of the car. The radio still played "The Beat Goes On" but we weren't going anywhere. We asked each other if we were "okay" and amazingly—we all were. We crawled out of the Hyundai and stood on the side of the road, giggling. The car's wheels still turned in the cold air, but the roof was smashed in and the engine had stopped running. There wasn't a scratch on us. Dad stood there holding all that was left of his coffee cup. His hand was bleeding a little. For a moment, he looked down at the broken mug handle, then tossed it in the ditch.

The first car to come by was a pickup truck and the shocked woman inside offered us a ride home. We all stood there for a moment, realizing that we'd be hopping in the back of her truck. We glanced at each other nervously. Sure, the ride was only a mile or so back to our house, but considering what had just happened it seemed risky. Dad, who had only months before taken us to the gravel pit up the road in his mustard-yellow Chevy Luv to cut cookies in the dirt, eyed the woman's truck with suspicion. "Okay," he said finally. "But take it easy and be careful. The roads are icy."

The flipping of the Hyundai marked a small cultural shift in our family unit: noting how close we'd come to death, we were forced to wear our seatbelts from that moment on. However, this change in our habits affected only one small portion of our family's general attitude, which was "having fun" combined with "God's will" finished off with a touch of "who gives a shit" that flirted on the edges of neglect as far as the seven of us offspring were concerned.

An entire case could be made for the presence of this attitude based solely on my parents' driving habits. Having outgrown every car we'd ever owned on account of God's skill at producing babies in my mother's stomach, my parents finally bought a one-ton church van that my mother drove as if it were a sports car. To top it off, the brakes were touchy and if Mom was going too fast we had the pleasure of experiencing our full gravitational heft towards the front of the vehicle when she applied the brakes. My mother was also an expert in multi-tasking while driving; this could include anything from applying make-up to praying in tongues, to—depending on the day, the destination, and the appetite or insistence of the infant-of-the-year—breast feeding. In fact, I often dreaded the coveted shotgun seat for this very reason. My mother would turn her co-pilot into a surgical assistant of sorts: she'd throw her bag of cosmetics onto my lap and require me to hand her the implements as she needed them. I would watch in horrified amazement as she curled her eyelashes or applied lipstick in the rearview mirror. Luckily, she had the whole regimen down to a science and was often applying the finishing touches of blush before we made it to the bottom of Loudon.

Not that my mother didn't care about our family's safety or the safety of others. Rather, much like the van she drove, her sense of danger had huge blind spots. I distinctly remember barreling over the narrow Sandy River Bridge in our minivan one summer. "You better get used to life in a wheelchair!" she screamed in the direction of two teenagers contemplating a jump into the rapids below. She then used her lightning-quick reflexes to avoid the oncoming traffic.

My father was only marginally better—by virtue of the fact that he didn't drive as often and never, as far as I know, wore makeup. He always had his full cup of coffee in one hand and usually seemed more interested in keeping it from spilling than avoiding catastrophe. Dad also discovered how fun it was for the seven of us to take turns standing behind him, covering his eyes while he drove down I-84 at 60 miles an hour.

Despite this reckless approach to driving and birth control, my mother won't ever admit to regret or wrongdoing. Perhaps for her, the mother of seven children, the stakes are too high to acknowledge even the tiniest doubt. But I don't want her to shrug my childhood off, to pass off my first eighteen years as a capricious folly.

My feelings towards her remain ambivalent. They dance between honor and accusation, awe and disdain. I was recently talking with her on the phone and told her that I had to get blood drawn at the doctor's the next day and wasn't looking forward to it. "I don't mind giving blood," my mother replied. "After you've had as many children as I have you're used to giving blood."

My mother gave birth to seven children: six girls and one boy. There would've been eight, but when I was eleven she miscarried. Two months into the pregnancy the nurse was unable to find a heartbeat and discovered that the baby had died. Our doctor knew we didn't have any health insurance and decided to send my mother home to miscarry. Keeping her in the hospital would've been expensive and most likely unnecessary. A day or so later she passed the baby into the toilet of our mobile home and called us in to say goodbye. My mother was nun-like and stoic above the toilet. "Say goodbye to Robin, you guys," she said. (She named the child Robin because we never knew the sex and this name could be applied to either.) We all looked down at the scarlet jellyfish in the toilet and mumbled a goodbye. I remember thinking that Robin was getting the funeral of a goldfish and wrestled with the idea of our shitty mobile home plumbing acting as some sort of conduit to heaven. My oldest sister Ana, sixteen at the time, suggested fishing Robin out of the toilet so we could decipher its sex, but Mom ruled against this and so we merely prayed and flushed the toilet. This was my first funeral. This also marked another kind of death: suddenly my mother's body no longer was the source from which all life effortlessly flowed.

Up until the miscarriage, I'd never conceived of a time when my mother would *not* be having babies. The family mythology is as follows: after giving birth to her fourth child, Zoe, my mother "gave it up to God," meaning she decided to stop using birth control. Zoe is the Greek word for life, and my mother's reproduction began to accelerate. Ever since I could remember, she'd always had a baby at her breast or been happily pregnant. I assumed that it would continue like this for all eternity.

This is not to say that I was not without my own doubts. When she got pregnant with my sister Simone so soon after Mikey was born, I found the pregnancy test in the bathroom garbage and confronted her. "Yes I'm pregnant," she said and went back to loading the dishwasher. With all the tact and dismay of a ten-year-old, I remember mumbling, "Already?"

I was worried about money. Having just been introduced to the public school system after a childhood of home-schooling, I'd become acutely aware of class difference. I couldn't help but notice which kids failed the lice checks, which kids were in the talented and gifted program, which kids got free lunches, which kids wore the nicest shoes. Shoes were a big deal. I was beginning to realize that my parents would never be able to afford even the minimum of orthodontia or new clothes for me or my siblings. But my parents, with their mysterious adult wisdom, didn't seem to mind this situation. It was "God's will" after all, all these babies. And that was the end of the conversation.

Yet, standing over the toilet that day, we witnessed a turning point in our conception of our mother's body. She was no longer an Edenic headwater. Her womb was fallible. This realization was somehow more disconcerting than the loss of little Robin, flushed out just moments before to the great beyond.

After we said our goodbyes, Mom lay down on the couch. And as the evening wore on, she kept bleeding. None of us noticed this. None of us noticed anything, really, until my mother visited the bathroom about half an hour later and remarked, "I'm still bleeding. I wonder if that's normal." She lay back down and Ana took over the dinner duties.

45 minutes later, my mother visited the bathroom again and remarked on the oddity of the situation. She returned to the couch. Her eyes rolled back in her head. "I wonder if something's wrong," she murmured. She fainted. Her blood had now soaked through her pants and was pooling on the towels underneath her on the couch.

Dad rushed over to her, yelling at us to put towels in the Hyundai and start it up. I watched through the kitchen window as he struggled to carry her limp frame down the porch steps and into the running car. Then they were off, Dad backing out of the driveway in a cloud of exhaust.

At the hospital it turned out my mother had lost nearly all the blood one can lose and still survive. They gave her a blood transfusion and a DNC to stop the hemorrhaging. All this we rehashed over the phone years later: how close she'd come to dying, how close we'd come to losing her. "What would your father have done?" my mother asked.

I thought about Robin's death and my mother's survival, the hypothetical lives that we as a family might have led.

"It would've been so hard on him," my mother continued.

It would've been hard on all of us, I thought.

Many years later, my oldest sister Ana confessed that while my parents were at the hospital she'd seriously contemplated dropping out of high school to take care of us. How even now she's angered by women who place their reproductive organs in God's hands. "What are you gonna do?" she asks in horror. "Keep having babies 'til you fall over dead?"

When my mother came home from the hospital she was struck by how needy we all were, how we gathered around her on the couch, the youngest only able to comprehend the fact of her absence—not the reason behind it. An economy-sized container of condoms soon appeared in my parents' bedroom and they never became pregnant again.

Only in retrospect did we realize that this was the third death in the story: Robin had died, my mother's fertility had died, but our *way of living* had also come to an end. Our universe had stopped expanding. The mad rush of fertility was over. Our family was now a closed club—no longer accepting new members. And although we never would have admitted it at the time, perhaps Robin was the ballast that kept our crowded little ship afloat.

"If you had died, our lives would've been so different," I said to my mother over the phone.

"What would we have done if we had lost me?" she said.

I understood what she meant. *What would we have done if we had lost me.* The question spoke to her inability to separate herself from the whole. I also have this inability. As a child, I felt secretly responsible for the reckless choices my parents made. I'm guessing my siblings did as well. What I've never been able to express to my mother is the profound guilt we all would've felt had she in fact died, had she quietly bled to death in our living room.

That night on the phone, my mother and I said our goodbyes and I got a glass of water and crawled into bed. As I fell asleep, my mind wandered out to Corbett once again, up the road into the mountains, past the broken-down fence at the bottom, past the steep bit where we got stuck in the snow, past the driveway where Dad was hit by a truck and broke his knee, and the corner where we flipped the Hyundai, up to the crest of the hill where Mom hit the pregnant doe in our brown Datsun, down the straight stretch where I'd steered with my knees, smoking pot from a little wooden pipe, and finally to where it dead-ended at our property, the mobile home and outbuildings scattered like some kind of white trash moon landing.

I can only imagine the speed at which my father raced down Loudon Road that night, with his wife of twenty years, the mother of his seven children, passing in and out of consciousness beside him in the passenger seat. Did he worry that he was going too fast, or not fast enough to save her life? As the Hyundai shook and teetered down Loudon, did he thank God that he'd already spent so many years driving this road like a madman?

Thanksgiving with Puppets

WE WERE HOME-SCHOOLED that autumn. We ate cake for breakfast, cereal for dinner. Mom tried to teach us long division, but it made us cry. Dad was unemployed. I was working on a novel about dragons. My oldest sister Ana studied Native Americans, Sarah studied whales, and little Zoe studied her dog and the best way to hide Mr. Goodbars, chocolate kisses, and bags of peas in the freezer.

One day, late in October, Ana said, "Maybe we should perform the Thanksgiving story with puppets?"

Thanksgiving was happening that year at my Aunt Linda's house, just down the dead-end country road from our house. Grandma Peaches and Step-Grandpa Ev were driving in from Gresham. I thought it was a bad idea. Linda's cooking was not my grandma's, and to make matters worse, our boy cousins all had food allergies of one sort or another.

While Sarah and Zoe were unenthusiastic, Ana and I seized on the puppet show idea. Finally we'd have a chance to express ourselves artistically. If we couldn't look forward to the food, at least we could look forward to putting on a show.

Besides, we'd all matured lately. Particularly little Zoe, who could now speak—and could no longer be relegated to the animal roles. On top of this, we now had a brother, Mikey, who in time might play the male roles, although we'd have to wait, since he was only two. Dramatic possibilities had expanded immensely. And I was always eager to show off for the relatives. The more we talked about it, the more Ana and I were, as Mom liked to say, "totally jazzed."

At the dining room table we made papier-mâché balloon heads for each of the puppets. First was the Pilgrim family—man, wife, the two kids—and then two Indians, both of them male. We sat for hours washing Cheez-Its down with Kool-Aid, chewing gluey newspaper strips into bits and applying the pasty substance in lumps and bumps onto the balloons. Voila, noses and ears. Sarah, by far the most skilled puppeteer, perfected this technique on the Indians' exaggerated Roman noses. The heads dried overnight.

In the morning we painted the heads. The Indians were easy: two coats of burnt sienna, some black eyebrows, and you were done.

"Maybe we should put some war paint on them," Sarah said, brush in hand.

"No. They're peaceful Indians," Ana replied. She was an expert on Indians now. Lately, she had been researching the Buffalo Dance and the Sun Dance, dramatic trials of human endurance and showmanship.

Zoe wandered in, her grubby hands full of the cedar rope we'd made last week from firewood. We'd done nothing else for a week but sit on top of the firewood pile at the lawn's edge and make yards and yards of cedar rope. We used some of it for the Indians' clothes.

The Pilgrims were more difficult to paint. Coat after coat of white paint did nothing to hide the newspaper underneath. Headlines about Ronald Reagan, the recession, and ads for Meier and Frank showed clearly through the white paint. After the fifth coat their skin was finally white enough to paint on thick red lips, blue eyes, and for the little girl and mother, bright yellow hair. The father and son were brunettes.

Ana and I got started on the script and in a week or so we had our lines down. Sarah and Zoe lost interest after the puppets were done. We had to force them to rehearse.

"Come on, you guys!" Ana said. "This is easy."

Zoe swayed nervously near the edge of the table. Dad was out-side in a tree yelling her name. He was hanging one last tire swing. With all his spare time from being unemployed, my father had been on a swing-hanging extravaganza since the summer.

At the moment, he was yelling to Zoe to bring him a glass of water up in the tree. Zoe faced a moral crisis. Whom to obey—Ana or Dad?

"Shhh. Zoe. Go hide in the bathroom." Ana was wearing her furry slippers with the claws on them, the ones that looked like Bigfoot. Zoe was forced to obey.

We sat and discussed the puppets as Dad yelled outside. "Zoe! Sarah! Martha!" His voice grew increasingly hoarse until it just trailed off.

Thanksgiving day we practiced the play three times. Ana and I would've liked to practice more but it was like pulling teeth to get the other two to concentrate. Sarah was always spacing out or sneaking off to look at whales in the piles of 1970's *National Geographics*. For the final rehearsal, Mom was our sole audience member, with little baby Simone in her arms. When it was over, she applauded and told us to hurry up and put on our coats.

We set the puppets down in a cardboard box, careful of their enormous heads and knobby ears, wrapped ourselves in a few layers, and walked out the door and down the road to Linda's house. Cats and kittens, some of them with odd-numbered toes, scattered as we approached the house.

Warm yellow light spilled out into the darkness along with Grand-ma's signature cackle and that strange "cousin's house" smell: a com-bination of boy smell, hints of laundry detergent, and cat dander.

"Everyone's eating already," Linda said, ushering us in. She brought us into the small living room and showed us the spread: half-eaten platters of canned vegetables, a few wieners in a simmer-ing crock pot, and the turkey was now all bony like a tree that had lost half its leaves. Camped unceremoniously on a paper plate were the dinner rolls—the white-flour perforated kind that come in groups of four and have to be torn away from their fellow rolls by force. This was the final blow. I'd thought at the least that Grandma would be bringing her famous bread.

Grandma Peaches and Step-Grandpa Ev were eating. Step-Grandpa Ev was drinking a beer. Somehow, it was even worse than we'd anticipated.

Cousins Tyler, Vincent, and Travis were running down the tiled hallway in their sock feet, slide-tackling the coat pile near the entry. Soon Dad was also eating, making terse conversation with his stepfather and Uncle Paul near the woodstove. Behind us, Mom carried infant Simone in a lighted crib because she had been born with jaundice.

Ana and I sat with the cardboard box full of puppets between us, guarding it from the boys.

The adults finished their food. So far, there'd been no mention of our puppet show. Did they even know we were going to be performing? Had my mother even told Grandma Peaches and Step-Grandpa Ev we had *handmade* these puppets? Ev got up to have a cigarette and get another beer.

Linda was fussing in the kitchen. Ana and I looked at each other. We were thinking the same thing: dessert first? Or our play? Ana whispered, "Someone should ask Mom about the show." She bugged her eyes at me.

I walked over to where my mother was nursing the baby and tugged on her sleeve. The baby tore its head away from her nipple. One string of milky saliva ran like a spider's web from the baby's mouth to my mother's breast. The baby had a glazed-over expression on its face. It stared at me, aware of my presence but not really seeing me, its gaping mouth all pink and toothless. Mom stared off into space. "Ana, could you get me a glass of water?" she said. I tugged on her sleeve again.

"What?"

"Our puppet show?" I whispered.

My mother looked at Linda. "Right. Everyone. The girls have a little play to perform."

Ev crossed his arms across his chest. Linda headed for the kitchen. "I'll pass out the pie," she said, "and you girls just get started." She pulled a tub of Cool Whip out of the fridge and set it next to the pumpkin pies on the counter. "Boys!" she yelled, " Pie!"

The boys slid into the living room. Travis walked over to the dish of mixed nuts and started throwing peanuts at my father. Dad pretended to start crying. "No, no, stop!" he said. "Please! Travis! Stop!" Travis thought this was hysterical. Grandma cackled. Seeing this, Tyler ran up to the dish full of nuts, dug out the macaroons and started chucking them as hard as he could at Dad's face. My father shielded himself with his hands. "Okay, okay," he said.

Uncle Paul's leg shot out at Travis from where he was sitting on the Lazy Boy. His son nearly fell over onto the coffee table. "Cut. It. Out."

I looked around for my sisters. Zoe and Sarah were hiding by the bookcase.

"Come on, you guys. We're gonna do it." Sarah reluctantly dug into the box of puppets and stuck an Indian and the little white boy on her hands. I was about to give Zoe her Indian when she said she had to pee and ran into the bathroom.

Ana rolled her eyes. "We can do it without her," she sighed, and put her hand on my shoulder. "We've done it before."

It suddenly occurred to us that we hadn't given thought to a stage. I peered anxiously around the living room.

As Linda passed out paper plates with pie, Sarah, Ana, and I pushed one couch away from the living room wall and crawled behind it. We stuck our puppeted hands up in the air.

"We can't see you!" yelled Grandma. We stuck our hands up higher.

Travis started shrieking. "I don't want cool whip!!" He became enamored with the sound of his own voice. It turned into a song. "I DON'T want cool whip! I don't WANT cool whip! I don't want COOL whip!"

"Shut up, Travis!" yelled my uncle. Vincent punched Travis in the stomach and they started wrestling.

"Cut it out!" Uncle Paul yelled from the corner.

Ana stood up. "Okay," she said. "This is the Thanksgiving story." She ducked back down.

I had the introductory line. "Way back when the Pilgrims came to America, they didn't know about food," I said.

Ana nudged Sarah. "They didn't know about turkey or popcorn," she blurted out.

"We can't hear you," Grandma said. "Speak up."

Sarah yelled, "They didn't know about popcorn!"

I popped my left arm up over the couch. "We're tired and hungry," the mother Pilgrim said meekly.

"What? What did you say?" Dad said.

"You guys are gonna have to speak up," Mom added.

"We're tired and hungry!" I yelled.

"This is interesting pie, Linda," I heard Grandma Peaches say.

Linda yelled over her shoulder from the kitchen, "I didn't put cinnamon in it. Tyler's allergic."

Ev grumbled something.

"We'll help you," said Ana's Indian, stretching his tiny arms wide.

I could feel our cousin Vincent kicking the couch now, slowly inching it backwards, pinning us against the wall.

"You guys, pay attention." Ana stood up and shook her head at the adults. She wagged her finger at them from inside the puppet, its big bobbly head seized and nodded.

Mom sighed audibly. "The couch is too thick. We can't hear you."

Sarah said up to Ana, "What's my line, now?"

"We'll just go to the part where they kill the turkey," Ana said.

This was the comic relief part. Or at least that's what Ana had called it. Our turkey was a drawing of a dead turkey, already cooked, a piece of tan paper on a popsicle stick. I'm not sure why we didn't make an actual living turkey, maybe because if it was already dead we wouldn't have to actually kill it, maybe because we wanted the Pilgrims to be able to eat immediately. Sarah's hand popped up with the turkey and she did a very good job of bobbing it up and down along the edge of the couch.

Nobody laughed at our already-dead turkey.

One of the kids started to cry.

Ana's mouth dropped.

"Okay. Don't worry about it," she said. "It's ruined now." Her face was stony and resolute.

I knew she was right. Ana and I sulked out from behind the couch. Sarah seemed relieved, and retreated to the bathroom with Zoe.

None of the adults even seemed to notice that we had abandoned our drama. The boys had already finished their pie and were shaking Mikey over the porch railing. Ev opened another beer and set it down next to his chair. He and Uncle Paul began talking about hunting. Dad stared off into space. I tried to eat some of the pie, but without the cinnamon it didn't taste right. Ana sat next to Mom and held the baby.

The boys ran in from outside and grabbed their toy guns out of the toy box in the hallway. "Look at this, Uncle Mike," Tyler said, and shot his rifle directly at my father. Dad instinctively grabbed for the gun and before either of them even knew what was happening they were engaged in a game of keep-away. Travis came up from behind and tried to get the gun from Tyler. Then Vincent tried to get the gun away from Tyler. I wasn't about to see someone get ganged up on, so I jumped on the couch behind Dad and put my hands over his eyes so he couldn't see. He fake screamed, "I'm blind. I'm blind. Martha, Martha, please stop!" We all thought this was hysterical.

With both hands wrapped around the handle of his toy gun, Tyler was pulling as hard as he could away from the couch. Ana, sensing an opportunity, crept up behind Tyler and picked him up, jerked him backwards. Dad, blinded and unaware, was pulled off the couch and brought to his knees on the floor. Instant dog pile. Ana, Tyler, Travis, Vincent, and I jumped on top of Dad, pushing him to the floor. Sarah and Zoe emerged from the bathroom and joined the pile.

Amid this froth of children, Dad kept trying to stand but was repeatedly brought to his knees. He would try to stand and push us over, but we kept bringing him back, our faces in the carpet. Someone was on top of me. I smashed Dad's head into the floor. He laughed.

"Get off," he said between laughs. "Okay, you guys. Stop now."

With Tyler on top of me, taking off his shoe, I caught a glimpse of Grandpa Ev. He was cracking another beer. Tyler hit Dad with his sneaker. Travis giggled wildly.

"Okay, you guys, get off me!" Dad pleaded. The boys laughed. "Get off!"

Dad fell silent. His head was on the ground, red veins bulging.

Then something hit me across the nose. My eyes stung. Tyler and Travis retreated and took off their shoes. Something hit me again on the back of the neck and I screamed. Ana was yelling. Zoe rolled away and started crying. Finally I realized that Dad had removed *his* shoe and was hitting us all indiscriminately with it. The shoe was a black outline of rubber. Thwack! I had never been hit in the face with anything, let alone my father's shoe. Sarah was on top of me and someone else was stepping on the back of my ankle. I screamed.

Hysteria.

"Stop it, Dad!" Ana yelled. He didn't. Now he was beating us all with his white tennis shoe. He got me again on the shoulder as I tried to escape.

All of us girls managed to get out of harm's way, but the cousins still were clamoring at our father as he tried to beat them away with his shoe.

Ana returned to the edge of the melee. "Child abuser!" she yelled, pointing her finger at my father. Grandma Peaches let out a loud guffaw.

I was crying. So was Zoe. Sarah and Ana were trying not to, but could barely contain themselves.

"You hit us in the face!" Ana said.

"You guys wouldn't get off me!" Dad's face was covered in sweat and the same color as the cranberry sauce.

"Are you hurt?" Grandma Peaches asked, her hands on her hips.

"No," Zoe sniffled. Sarah and I broke down into sobs.

"Why did you hit us?" we wanted to know.

Grandma snapped. "He told you already, Martha," she said. "You wouldn't listen." Uncle Paul was shaking Travis in the corner. He said something very quiet to Travis that I couldn't hear. Travis started crying and Paul shook him harder. Ev tried to hide a grin.

My father laughed uncomfortably.

"I hate you!" Ana screamed at my father.

I looked around. Mom was sitting silently in the corner with the baby. Linda was sending her sons to their rooms. Vincent was standing in his open doorway, throwing a pink rubber ball against the hallway wall. I wanted to say I hated them all, too, every single last one of them, even Mom, even the baby. I said nothing.

"We're leaving," Ana said. And that was it. I realized we had the tool of silence in our tool kit, the tactic of retreat. We gathered up the puppets, followed Ana down the hall, put on our coats, walked out into the cold night. Zoe was crying. We put our arms around her. Sarah and I held hands.

On the way home we composed a song. Zoe and I had been into Mother Goose the previous summer and were pretty good at rhyming. The song was almost complete by the time we got home. Sarah added harmony. Ana punctuated the last refrain with a fist against the starry night.

We walked down our driveway and let ourselves into the empty mobile home. We practiced some more in the living room until all of us knew the words.

By the time Mom and Dad got home an hour later, we had raided the fridge and were finishing off Dad's Neapolitan ice cream, the box of puppets beside us on the living room floor.

"We have written a song," Ana said. She got up and put her arms across her chest. "That you have to listen to."

Mom and Dad sat down obediently.

We stood in a row in front of them and sang our song.

"What's a poor girl to do?

"When her father hits her with a shoe, a shoe?

"What's ZOE to do?"

(Zoe steps out front and holds up her arms.)

"When her own Dad makes her black and blue?

"We're abused!!

"We're abused!!"

(This part only Ana sings)

"What can they really teach you

When your own father beats you?"

We sang it loud and with feeling. Mom grinned, awake for the first time all night. Dad clapped and said it was well written. He sat there on the couch with a strange smile on his face.

Clear Cut

I'M THIRTEEN. My family stands together on the deck of the mobile home. One after another, to the whining dirge of the chainsaws, the trees of my childhood are cut.

I was recently on the phone with my dad and he told me he heard on the news that three local high school students were rushed to the hospital because they'd eaten poisonous hemlock.

"Someone told them it was wild parsley!" my father grunted in disbelief. "I mean, I wouldn't eat anything that someone told me was a wild-whatever. Unless it was a wild Snickers bar."

"Really?" I said. "I would've. As a child I ate stuff all the time that people told me was edible. I ate huckleberries and sour grass and other stuff."

My dad grew quiet on the other end of the phone. "Man, I wish I'd had a better idea of what you were and were not eating."

Although he expresses regret about it now, it was my parents' very laissez faire attitude that made childhood so spectacular. This, along with my home-schooling, pretty much guaranteed that from ages six to twelve I would spend every day in the woods behind our house. Whole weeks went by without any math work getting done. We rubbed our faces black with the ashy wood from this one particular stump—a blackened relic from an ancient forest fire. We decorated our faces with clay. We ran through patches of stinging nettle. We climbed trees and fell out. We got concussions, rashes, scrapes, cuts. In the meantime, we were in continuous warfare with the neighborhood boys and never passed up the opportunity to make the weakest among them cry.

I don't remember my parents going into the woods very often. Sometimes my father would cut down a tree here or there for firewood. He would bribe us with trips to a local pool if we hauled it out piece by piece in the summer heat.

By the sixth grade I'd developed an almost unhealthy fantasy life that made my woods into a kind of private fairyland. My pockets were packed with tokens, amulets, and bottles of colored sand. The woods were both familiar and exotic. Depending on the day and the season, they could be a fairyland, a jungle, the wilds of Europe, or simply "the woods." Using the deer trails, my sisters and I built forts all over the property. We gave names to every bend and hill; every tree had a personality, a spirit, a story.

And then, in 1993, my family, dead-broke and desperate, logged our property and prepared to move to Wisconsin to run a restaurant.

A videotape arrived from Wisconsin in a large manila envelope. We'd been waiting for it for weeks and we all gathered around the TV and put it in the VCR. Heavy breathing. A slight nasal intake, as though one nostril were plugged, and then the voice: laboring, resigned. A Wisconsin accent said, "Well, this is the restaurant. This is the north view and the parking lot."

The tape went black. We found ourselves in a steep, dark stairwell. The lungs labored up the stairs and into a narrow hallway. "This is the apartment," they said. "As you can see, there are rooms on either side. Eight rooms total."

The hallway was cramped. Several overloaded bookcases were propped outside the doors. To the right was the living room: a couch, a TV, stacks of boxes. Then the bedroom: a double bed with a maroon blanket, lace curtains, more boxes. There was no kitchen, only a bathroom with a microwave on the counter. Two dirty cereal bowls rested in the sink. More boxes.

The whole upstairs apartment, where we would be living, was used as much for storage as it was for living: storage of stuff—boxes and boxes of it—and the storage of two bodies, one of which, the one holding the camera, seemed too tired to provide even minimal enthusiasm for its surroundings.

A cursory tour of the restaurant downstairs and the screen turned black. That was that. We prepared to move. Put the house on the market. Cut down the trees.

And our three-bedroom mobile home sat on the market. Sat on the ravaged land over the summer. It didn't sell.

Years later, my father tells me that no one is going to hell for clear-cutting five acres. I know he's right—in the grand scheme of things, and even in the wisdom of forest ecology, our tiny plot of earth was pretty insignificant. The acreage we logged was comparable to a naturally occurring wildfire. And we followed the rules: we replanted, we respected the riparian zone. If hell exists, I don't think we'll enter its gates on account of the clear cut.

I'm glad we didn't move to Prentice, Wisconsin, to run a restaurant. In hindsight, much of my life hinges on the decision to stay. But I find myself thinking about Prentice sometimes. The six of us girls: small town waitresses. My father would've had to get up every morning at 5:00 a.m. to snow-blow the parking lot. And my father is not this type of man. (My father counters that he *is* this type of man. That he would've done it but he "wouldn't have liked it.")

The two decrepit logging trucks which showed up on our gravel driveway that spring said "Prentice" in silver metal on their grills. Turns out the only real industry in Prentice is the manufacture of logging equipment. In three days of manic chain-sawing, the loggers took every tree worth taking. I don't remember the men. I have no memory of their faces, their clothes. If they even spoke to us. But I can't forget the whine of the blades through the trees, the crash of each trunk. When a Douglas Fir falls, it momentarily resembles a palm tree, the way the crown of the tree seems to throw up its hands in panic or ecstasy.

81 SYMPTOMS

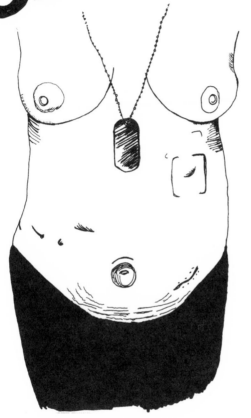

Palm Reader

AT OUR FIRST APPOINTMENT the endocrinologist asks me to show her some scars.

"I don't really have any scars," I say, not thinking about it too hard. "Except this one from a fight Sarah and I got into when I was like ten."

I show her the small crescent-shaped scar on my right hand and smile at my sister Sarah sitting in the chair to my left. She's come with me to this appointment for moral support. Dr. B turns my hands over and examines the scar as if she's a palm reader.

"I also have some chicken pox scars on my face from when I was a kid," I say, "but yeah—I don't have very many scars."

But now, sitting on the examination table, facing these questions, the fact that I don't have any scars seems strange to me. Why don't I have any scars? It's not as if I've been a knife juggler, or a rugby player, or anything, but I *have* worked in a kitchen since I was fifteen and have had my fair share of cuts and burns. I stare down at my hands—they're pristine. Do I have some superhuman healing ability I'm unaware of?

A faint smile flutters across Dr. B's face. She's staring intently at me. What does she see? She pulls back my thinning hair and silently examines the few tiny chicken pox craters on my forehead.

"Do you have an old picture of yourself? An old license photo?"

She takes her index fingers and presses on my collarbone and the small hump at the back of my neck.

"My license photo is from a couple months ago," I answer. I know what she's getting at. She wants to see a before and after comparison. She wants to see how much and in what way I've gained weight.

The doctor looks from one of us to the other. "Well the two of you don't look like sisters. Your face is round. Hers isn't so round—it's more oval."

But us Grover girls look like twins. Nobody's ever told me I don't look like one of my sisters. She says there are a couple more tests I have to take and they will call me with the results.

By the time Sarah and I get down to my car in the hospital garage, I'm sweating all over. My hands are shaking. Dr. B and the intake nurse asked me so many questions. Do you have headaches, do you have insomnia, when was your last period. And the whole thing about the scars.

Sarah sits in the passenger seat. I get behind the wheel and start driving the wrong way out of the parking garage. "What do you think?" I ask, turning to my sister.

"When you got up and left to go the bathroom," Sarah answers, "Dr. B told me that she knew you had Cushing's Disease the minute you walked in the door."

An SUV comes around the corner and nearly hits us. The driver honks.

"Can you drive us home?" I say.

81 Symptoms

CUSHING'S DISEASE:

A hormonal disorder characterized by an excess of cortisol, the body's stress hormone. Rare and under-diagnosed, the disease can cause heart attacks, diabetes, depression, psychosis, and death.

SYMPTOMS:

facial redness
thinning of the hair
sudden weight gain
facial rounding
abdominal fat
hump of fat at the back of neck
thinning of arms and legs
low resistance to infections
sensitivity to sun
oily skin
dry skin
fragile, thin skin
excessive sweating
osteoporosis
osteoarthritis
spreading of the teeth

weakness in the legs
weakness in the arms and hands
severe fatigue
low energy
muscle weakness
unexplained fractures
carpal tunnel syndrome
numbness or tingling in arms and legs
puffy eyes
dry eyes and mouth
blurred vision
hair growth on chin, chest, and back
hair loss on scalp
heart palpitations
premature aging of the blood vessels
high blood sugar
high blood pressure
chest pain
depression
anxiety
short-term euphoria
hallucinations
irritability
mood swings
disorientation
difficulty concentrating
memory lapse
cognitive lapse
lethargy
insomnia
lack of restful sleep
snoring
sleep apnea

kidney stones

glucose intolerance

diabetes

hormone problems associated with water retention

nausea

vomiting

constipation

dizziness

loss of balance

vertigo

headaches

chronic bacterial infections

electric shock sensation under the skin

bleeding gums

pain with urination

irritable bowel syndrome

incontinence

indigestion

gas pain

brittle nails and hair

irregular periods

absent periods

infertility

tremors

minimal scarring

easy bruising

dark tanning

skin tags

skin rashes

changes in body odor

changes in vision

If left untreated, Cushing's Disease will kill me in five to ten years.

First Scar

"Now I don't want you to get on the Internet and get yourself all freaked out about the different symptoms," says Dr. B at our next meeting. "Don't get on the chat rooms and read all those horror stories. Those people just like to whine and vent. It will only stress you out." She lets out a big sigh and rolls herself up to the computer. "Now," she says, squinting at the screen, "I know some very good surgeons here at this hospital and up at OHSU. We're going to remove the tumor from your pituitary and you'll be good as new."

I've already found a whole community of "Cushies," as they call themselves, on the Internet, on various websites, sharing their stories and generally commiserating. Every night I pour over their tales and soon find myself fixating on all the different symptoms. There are 81 in all. I have some of these already: weight gain, osteoporosis, hair loss, hypoglycemia, irregular period, tremors, excessive sweating. But there it is: minimal scarring! It seems the only positive symptom on the whole list. I don't scar!

I sit in front of my laptop and walk backward through my life. All those years with a butcher knife in front of a prep sink, cutting bok choy and romaine, spinning around in a crowded kitchen with slopping pans of grease and sizzling steak platters, backing up into other waiters, my hands full of steaming bread and soup—no scars.

Alone in my apartment, I examine my arms and hands. Nothing. Not a mark. Nothing from all those years, all that contact with heat and steel.

My first brain surgery is scheduled at Oregon Health Sciences University. Officially it's called a transphenoidal pituitary resection. None of my friends or family understands these words, of course, so I find myself calling it a brain surgery. The surgeon is going to go up through my nose with a microscope and remove the tiny tumor and drag it down through my nasal cavity. No drill, no bone saw. Basically no cutting, except for the tiny perforation at the back of my nose. After they remove the tumor, my cortisol levels will normalize, my body's hormones will right themselves and I will be cured.

All done—good as new.

Two months later I sit in the neurosurgeon's office with my mother. The first word out of his mouth is "bummer." I've gained twenty pounds. He sits there for a moment and we stare at each other. We schedule another surgery.

I wake in the hospital bed with cotton up my nose and an incision on my belly. My second failed surgery. My first scar.

Fat

THE SCALE TELLS ME that I've gained 70 pounds, but it's my pants that tell me I'm fat.

The pants that I tried on a couple of weeks ago, the ones that were a little too snug to be flattering, now I can't even get them over my thighs. I can't button my shirts. Sometimes I can't even get my biceps through the sleeves.

My body has new parts that it never had before. New rolls, new sub-parts, addendums to my former self. I now have back fat. The weird thing about back fat is that when you turn around it's like someone is touching you. You feel this crease, this pinch, and you're like *who is that?* But it's just you. It's just your self touching yourself. *Hey there*, your self says to yourself, and your shocked self replies *fuck you*.

I've now got the gut.

Every woman has a little gut, but I'm talking about an actual gut. Like a stomach that folds over my jeans no matter how loose they are. Beneath that is another fold, like a postscript to the gut. Although it's more discrete, the postscript gut is far more disgusting than the actual gut: this marks the beginning of a collection of rolls that I want with all my might to stop—a card file of flesh, a Dewey Decimal system of fat. Now I have to buy big underwear to minimize the friction. My pants wear out in the crotch and I have to take this hot spot into consideration in my shaving and moisturizing regimens.

My feet hurt more, my back hurts more, I become winded more easily. I avoid bending over, looking down. And even though I'm fatter, for some reason I have to pull up my pants more often.

And then I think about that time long ago when I lost twenty pounds—the thighs I admired as I whipped through town like a spider, my chin like a dagger, my hip bones jutting ridges.

It's like remembering myself as a different person, like touching a statue draped in wool.

Fourth MRI

THEY TAKE THE HAIR tie from my hair. The tech with the southern accent tells me that its small metal fastener will burn a hole right through my skull. He locks my head into the head brace. "You look like Darth Vader," he says. "Or wait, the brace is white, so really you're a storm trooper."

I try not to think about how often he tells that joke.

"I told that joke earlier today," he tells me, "and the girl was like fifteen and she didn't know what I was talking about. 'Didn't you see *Star Wars?*' I said." He throws up his arms. "She'd never seen *Star Wars!*"

"Wow!" I say—as if that's even more amazing than what I am about to undergo. The tech gives me the squeezy thing in case I panic and goes behind the glass on the other side of the MRI room. He pushes a button or pulls a lever or clicks a mouse, whatever they do behind the glass, and my body moves up and backwards into the tube. This MRI machine is the smallest one yet and a brisk stream of air starts pumping over my face. On the one hand, it's nice to have fresh air, but on the other, it's so cold I can't relax or fall asleep, which is what I would like to do.

It's 10:30 p.m. This is my last appointment of the day. I've had my blood pressure taken, blood drawn, I've dropped off nearly two gallons of my urine, been weighed, hooked up to an EKG, gotten a bone density test, had my knees knocked with the reflex hammer, done balance tests, gotten my glands checked, my throat looked at, my ears checked, and now at this late hour I've been scheduled for an MRI.

When I got here tonight, the hospital was locked. The tram had stopped running. The parking lots were empty and their blackened puddles reflected the eerie red glow of emergency signs. Most of the surgeons were gone for the day. Left were the nurses, the janitors, the security guards, the blue-collar workers of the hospital.

Yet even at this late hour, it's been a madhouse in the MRI facility. When I am called into the back room I walk through the double doors and see a woman in a hospital bed directly in front of me. I can't tell if she is awake or asleep. The IV nurse apologizes that there isn't a more comfortable chair and sets me up in an office chair next to a computer and puts in my IV.

She disappears into the next room and I wait there with the needle sticking out of my arm. The woman in the hospital bed begins stirring and I see that her eyes are open. After a couple minutes, two techs come out and start talking to the woman on the bed. Apparently she's wearing a back brace and they have to remove it before she can get an MRI. The woman seems very drugged-up and she keeps trying to "help" them as they remove the brace. They keep telling her to relax. The woman is practically immobile but she keeps trying to sit up. I can't stop cringing as they remove the brace and move her onto a gurney. She disappears into the next room.

An antsy woman waits by the door of the bathroom to my left. She has that thin, scarred look of a heavy drug user and smoker. She can't stop moving around and shivering. After a couple of minutes a woman in a gown comes around the corner and changes in the bathroom. They leave together.

A door opens to my right and I realize that there is an elevator shaft almost directly behind me. A nurse's assistant wheels in an unconscious woman on a hospital bed, smiles at me, and leaves. The woman snores loudly. I watch the clock.

The unconscious woman starts moaning and moving around on the bed. Her blanket falls off and pretty soon one leg is hanging mid-air. I look around. No nurses in sight. One of the lady's blue, fuzzy slippers falls onto the ground and I'm afraid that she might ... I don't know what I'm afraid of, actually.

I get up with my IV dangling from my arm and walk into the back room. There are two nurses talking by a computer console. "Hi," I say. "This lady out here is waking up. She lost her shoes." I'm not sure why I'm telling them this.

One of the nurses hops up and follows me back into the waiting room where the unconscious woman is still moaning. Both slippers are on the floor now. The nurse picks up the slippers and covers her with the hospital blanket.

"Where is her chart?" she says.

The nurse disappears again into the back room. That's when I'm called back to my MRI. Afterwards I walk back out into the waiting room and there are nearly a dozen surgeons having a heated conversation around an unconscious patient on a gurney. Something has gone wrong in surgery. I have to weave my way through them to get my purse and jacket. "Excuse me," I say.

As I make my way out of the hospital, I pass a janitor running the Zamboni along the empty hallway. I finally reach my car in the garage. I'm surprised by my competence and composure: being able to laugh at the tech's joke, managing to face the unknown. A few weeks ago my gall bladder surgeon patted me on the shoulder and called me a "trooper." And I feel silly for feeling so proud of myself. Sometimes I just wish I was unconscious like that woman kicking off her slippers.

Drug Study

I SHOW UP at OHSU's Pituitary Center with only black coffee and antidepressant in my stomach. The research assistant and Nurse Y come into the exam room and on the examination table they display what will be my new companions for the next six months: needle heads, syringes, cotton bandages, alcoholic wipes, a blood sugar monitor, strips for the blood sugar monitor, a lancet gun, and my drug study folder. They bring in two boxes of sealed glass vials (the experimental drug) and stack them on the table. They tell me to take the medicine twice daily—once in the morning and once at night, between eleven and thirteen hours apart. I must pierce my finger with the lancet gun and record my blood sugar level a few hours after each injection.

Nurse Y shows me how to assemble the syringe and sterilize the injection site. She takes a glass vial the size of a locket out of the box and shows me the little blue dot on its neck. "Face this dot away from you," she says, "and use your index finger to flick any air bubbles to the top of the vial." She flicks the vial several times until all the medication slides to the bottom, then grabs a cotton bandage and covers the neck of the vial. She pulls the neck of the vial towards herself until we hear a pop and the neck breaks off. She throws the bandage and the glass top into the garbage. Then, with one hand, she holds the vial and inserts the needle into the clear liquid. With her other hand, Nurse Y pulls up the plunger on the syringe until the liquid starts to fill the barrel. She periodically removes the syringe and flicks it, sending any air bubbles to the top of the barrel. She depresses the plunger and pushes the air out. She repeats this process until all the medication is gone from the vial.

"I'll do one injection and you can do the next," she says.

Nurse Y pulls up my shirt.

I'm wearing my bright orange sweatshirt. It's become my favorite article of clothing. It's construction orange. I found it on the sidewalk. Nurse Y pulls my skin flat, to one side, and plunges the needle in. I don't feel anything. She shows me how to pull backwards slightly with the plunger to make sure I haven't hit a vein and then she injects me with the medication. She pulls the needle out and that's it. "Your turn," she says.

I repeat the steps she's shown me and pull up my shirt. I'm surprised at how the tiny needle bounces off my skin at first, but now on the second try it goes in and I inject myself with the second dose of medication. When I pull out the needle, several drops of medication ooze out of my skin. "That's why you have to pull your skin to one side," says Nurse Y. "So that when you let it go, the skin covers the injection site."

Dr. F comes into the room and starts to talk to me about the drug study. She periodically stops and asks me how I'm doing.

"I'm fine," I say.

The doctors leave the room. I dig into my purse and pull out the Pringles can and the Powerade I fished off the floor of my car this morning in the parking garage. These OHSU visits are always in the morning and I'm always having to fast for the blood draws. Now I'm starving. I cram a couple of handfuls of Pringles into my mouth followed by a swig of bright orange Powerade.

Dr. F and Nurse Y come back into the room and ask me how I'm doing. "I'm great," I say.

But then suddenly I'm not so great. The room starts to slant.

Dr. F veers to the left. "I feel sick," I say. "I feel like I'm going to throw up," I say.

Nurse Y rips open an alcohol swab and holds it under my nose. "Take a deep breath," she says. It smells awful and I'm not sure what this is supposed to accomplish. The research assistant runs down the hall and grabs a bucket for me. All three of them leave the room and turn off the light.

I throw up three times into the bucket. The first is bright orange Powerade, the second is the Pringles, and the third time I throw up, I taste something bitter. It must be my antidepressant.

Thai Massage

THE STEPS DOWN to the massage parlor beneath the Thai restaurant are wet. Blinds are drawn over two small windows. Before I get the door even halfway open, an older woman pulls it wide from the other side. "You want massage?" she asks, grabbing my free hand.

She pulls me into a dark and very warm basement room. It's so dark inside that I can barely make out the couch where she's been sitting and the decorations on the wall. Some gray light seeps in from one window. Daytime talk shows scream from a huge TV. Another woman sits on the couch, her shadow a darker gray against the back wall of the room.

The older woman leads me into a side room. "Take everything off," she says and sweeps her hands over her body to illustrate. She hurries out of the room and I start undressing.

She comes right back as I'm taking off my bra and asks me if I need help. "I'm fine," I say. She instructs me to take off my underwear too, but I tell her that I'd rather keep them on.

It seems like something is missing, some hippie ceremony. Why isn't she telling me, as she turns on the sound of rain and humpback whales on a boom box, to "get comfortable" and "take my time?"

The woman's English isn't very good. As I climb up on the table I ask her to avoid my stomach because I've just had a surgery and it's still a little tender.

"You have surgery?" she asks.

"Yes," I say face-down into the table. "I had my gall bladder removed."

"In your legs?" She's on top of the table now pressing down on my back.

"No, in my stomach."

The woman hasn't bothered to turn off the TV and through the open door I hear the next case being brought before Judge Judy. "Let me get this straight," says Judge Judy. "You let this woman move in with you, not knowing anything about her except what you learned on Craigslist?"

I can't hear the plaintiff's response.

"You no work today?" asks the masseuse.

I don't feel like making conversation. Not only because she doesn't know where the gall bladder is but also because I just don't feel like it. I walked down here with my cane and I'd rather just space out and try to forget about being sick for a while. "No," I say. "I just thought a massage sounded nice."

The woman leaves. Through the open door I hear a man's voice murmuring something. The other woman goes into a room with the man. And the TV is still on. My masseuse returns with a hot towel and places it on my back and starts slapping my body with her hands. "You ever have Thai massage?" she asks.

"No," I say.

"Let me get this straight, you smashed a beer bottle and shoved it in your friend's face?"

"No. I don't know. I fell."

"You were drunk."

"I was—"

"Let me finish—I'm the judge, it's my turn to talk. You were stumbling around drunk and you blacked out and cut your friend's face with a beer bottle. How many stitches did you have to have?"

"Thirteen, Your Honor."

The woman stops slapping my back. "It's over," she says.

I know it hasn't been an hour yet. "I'm sorry?"

"Turn over," she says.

"Oh, turn over. I'm sorry, I didn't understand you." I turn over. I hear her gasp. She's seen my Frankenstein scar from my second brain surgery and the scattershot scars from my recent gall bladder surgery.

"Oh," she says. "I only do circulation."

I grunt in agreement although I'm not sure what she means by this.

The masseuse begins stroking my stomach with her hands, tracing the contours of my torso. I don't know where to look. Up at her face seems wrong. Maybe the ceiling? Or should I close my eyes? I end up staring at the dim light bulb in the ceiling. A commercial's on now for a business college. The woman runs her index finger around my belly button. I want to tell her to stop but I don't want to be rude. Her finger is going around and around as if circling a drain. Is this supposed to be relaxing? I start to feel my nipples get hard, exposed as I am, cold. I wonder if this is where she would offer a male client a hand job, and then I feel bad for assuming that she is a sex worker, assuming anything—that she doesn't like her job, that she is passive, that she is a victim. I glance up at her face and she is spacing out, staring at the wall. She looks bored.

"Unemployed? In a dead-end job? Have you ever considered a career in the medical field?"

"You want a shower?" She motions towards the corner of the room. I don't want to take off any more of my clothes, which at this point is just my underwear. I just want to leave. I put my clothes back on over my shivering, oily body. I pay her and walk back out into the cold. It's now as dark outside as it was in the massage parlor. On the way back to my friend's house, I duck into a fancy boutique to warm up. The two skinny white women working there ignore me.

Specimen

AFTER I DROP off two jugs of urine at the lab, the study coordinator and I ride the tram down the hill to the Pituitary Center. I'm wearing my orange sweatshirt again. It's my favorite sweatshirt. It's bright construction orange and I figure if it becomes my "OHSU uniform" I won't have to worry about the doctors making jokes about it.

I walk into the examination room and Nurse Y is there with another doctor who I don't recognize. "Martha, this is Dr. S," she says. "Do you mind if we use this as a learning experience?"

"Not at all," I say. And I really don't mind. I've had enough experience with OHSU to know that nearly every procedure here is a learning experience for someone. I'm finally settling into my role as a medical oddity. The already small pool of people who have gone through what I'm going through shrinks day by day, what with the failed surgeries, the adverse reactions, the strange and arbitrary combination of symptoms. There have been only 150 participants in this international study, and the study is in its fourth year.

It usually doesn't bother me that OHSU is a teaching hospital, but there are moments. Once, during a post-surgery visit with the ear nose and throat doctor, the doctor asked if I minded if one of his interns sat in on the examination and subsequent "de-boogering" session. I didn't mind. But after the doctor stuck the scope up my nose, the intern attached what I can only describe as something out of a Terry Gilliam movie to one end of the scope and looked into it. The doctor proceeded to point out the various parts of my nasal cavity: the incision, the swelling, everything. And there I was, trying not to cry, trying not to mess up my mascara while the doctor went on and on and the intern murmured in agreement. I felt wholly unpresent. I felt myself hovering in space, waiting for them to be done.

And now, in the examination room, I smile at Dr. S and Nurse Y and it's their turn to be uncomfortable. I have no idea who this doctor is. I can only assume she is someone that is interested in seeing this "specimen," this medical oddity. But now here I am, a real live person, not a picture in a medical book.

I stand in front of Nurse Y and she points out the physical markers of Cushing's Disease one by one. "You'll see here," she says, "the moonface. Facial rounding." She looks into my eyes. "Hopefully that will go away soon."

Nurse Y presses down on the back of my neck. "As you can see, she has a little bit of a buffalo hump, a fatty deposit at the back of her neck. And fatty deposits on her neck." She pulls down my sweatshirt and shows Dr. S my nonexistent collarbone. "Also, facial redness and acne." She furrows her brow. "Although you don't have much acne."

"Nope," I say. "I never had much in high school and I don't have much now. Why is that?"

Nurse Y shrugs. She points at my belly. "You'll also see how most of her obesity is around her midsection and her limbs are relatively thin. Her weight pattern isn't terribly exaggerated. You should see some people, they come in and their arms and legs are—"

"Like apples on a stick?" I say.

"Yes, like apples on a stick," says Nurse Y and we both laugh. Dr. S looks uncomfortable.

The nurse pulls down my pants at the waistline and shows Dr.

S the red stretch marks growing like wildfire up the side of my hips. "You'll see striae here. And sometimes they'll get them on the breasts and legs."

I cheerfully tell Dr. S that I have them all over my breasts and down my thighs all the way to my knees.

I want to tell her that I don't mind that much, that the stretch marks on my breasts look like dahlias radiating out from my nipples, that I know that the splotchy stretch marks on my thighs will mellow to a translucent abalone. I want to tell her that what I hate is my belly, that it gets in the way, that it's a perverse overhang. That it's growing so baroque I feel like a pug dog and if it gets any worse will soon have to clean my abdomen with a q-tip to ward off yeast infections. I want to tell her what it's like to live in and out of my body every day, how it feels to lie in bed and rest my hands on thighs that are slowly wasting away, on a butt that slacks away from the rest of me like a deflating balloon.

But I don't. We move on to a physical test. Nurse Y grabs my hands and asks me to resist as she pushes down on them. She easily pushes down my hands. "I also make them sit down and stand up several times," she says to Dr. S. "Most Cushing's patients have a hard time doing this."

I nod at Dr. S. "I can't do that very well," I say. Dr. S doesn't seem to like the fact that the specimen keeps talking to her.

And suddenly we're done with the show-and-tell portion of the visit. "Nice to meet you," Dr. S says, and leaves.

The study coordinator comes back into the room with a big grocery sack full of my next round of meds and syringes. Nurse Y and I talk about my hives and diarrhea, my blood sugar, my aches and pains. I ask Nurse Y if she can prescribe me some pain meds.

She frowns. "Unfortunately I can't. You'll have to ask your regular doctor about that."

I start to ask her about osteoporosis medication and suddenly, I can't remember what I'm saying. I don't know if I'm here. I can't locate myself. I wonder if this is actually happening to me. Nurse Y looks like a stranger. I stutter through my question and then the feeling is gone and I'm here. It's December 2008, I'm on the eighth floor of the Center of Health and Healing at OHSU, it's 9:30 a.m., and I'm in examination room number thirteen. I'm somewhere between illness and recovery and the study coordinator is drawing my blood.

Cane

IF MY RIGHT SIDE hurts, I hold the cane with my left hand. If my left side hurts, I hold it with my right. The cane and my bum leg stride in tandem. If both sides hurt? That's what painkillers are for.

I have an adjustable, lightweight cane, and I find myself throwing it around, jaunty-like. I can also use the cane to open doors that have that special disabled button on them.

Certain situations present certain problems: getting out of a car is especially hard for me and has taken some practice. What makes this difficult is that both the steering wheel and the car door move back and forth as I try to pry myself out of the sitting position. The door flops around, and unless I lock it, the wheel turns. Low-to-the-ground couches are also difficult.

People treat you differently when you have a cane. They're nicer: they open the door, they get out of your way. They offer to carry things for you. The cane legitimizes your illness.

It's for these reasons that I carry my cane even when I don't need it.

A cane says—I mean business.

Disability Lawyer

AND THERE IS a business behind all of this: my business of being sick is the business of my disability lawyer.

I climb the stairs to the disability lawyer's office with my cane. I'm wearing my back brace. His office is located above a tanning salon at the top of a steep flight of stairs. I worry that he might be weeding out his best clients with this location, but I wheeze up the stairs anyway. It's a small office—a couple rooms down a short hallway. There's no receptionist and I look around for a bathroom. The lawyer sees me wandering around the foyer and comes out to greet me. He's wearing a shirt, a tie, a green sweater, and a tweed dress jacket. He seems overdressed, but I guess it is a little cold in here. I ask to use the bathroom and he gives me the key. It's attached to a spoon with a paper clip.

When I return, we sit down at his desk and the lawyer explains the process to me: you apply for disability and they turn you down, you apply again and they turn you down, and then you apply for a hearing and two years later they may turn you down again. Then he goes on about federal court and this court and that court and I can feel my eyes glaze over. I file the information in the "doesn't matter right now" file. Perhaps in the future it will move to the "may never matter" file.

The lawyer takes out a legal pad and asks me what kind of work

I do, whether I went to high school, if I have any kids. We get into logistics about how much weight I can lift, how long I can stand, how long I can sit.

"Have you taken any long trips recently?" he asks.

"Define long," I say.

"To the beach."

"I went to Seattle with my grandpa a couple weeks ago," I say.

"How was that?"

I think about it for a while. My grandpa ran laps around me. I spent most of the trip in bed, watching cable TV in the hotel room. Our one foray into the city was to the art museum and my back was killing me after about twenty minutes of standing. "It wasn't great," I say.

"Are you being treated for anxiety and depression?" he asks.

"That's what the Lexipro is for," I say. "And I was seeing a therapist until recently but I had to stop because I couldn't afford it anymore."

He looks up from his notepad, "Self worth?" he says.

"I think I'm pretty awesome." I know he just has a box to check, but healthy people can be so condescending. I remind myself that this man is on my side.

"How's your social life?"

"It's not as good as I'd like. I don't go out much anymore. I don't volunteer or socialize much. I can't make commitments when my health is so up and down. I have diarrhea, my blood sugar crashes constantly and I'm tired all the time—"

"Diarrhea?"

"Every day. And I mean—I've gained 70 pounds, I've stopped having my period, I've started growing facial hair." I raise one hand off my cane into the empty air. "I don't even know if I'll be able to have children—

"—so I guess—my self-image, not my self worth, has changed. Maybe I don't go out so much because of that. I can't go out past

8:00 at night because I have to take my medicine at 9:00. I have to inject it into my stomach."

He's scribbling things down on his paper. I wonder if he's writing "facial hair."

"You're not purposefully isolating yourself?" he asks.

"No. Not on purpose."

"Suicide?" he says without looking up.

"I don't have a plan or anything. I wouldn't say I'm suicidal but I do think about it—if I'm being honest."

The lawyer takes off his glasses and rubs the bridge of his nose. "A lot of my clients who are dealing with chronic illness think 'Yeah, it would be great to go to sleep and never have to deal with this again.' Is that what you mean?"

"Yeah." I swallow. "That's basically where I'm at."

"Anxiety. What situations give you anxiety?"

"Hmm. Driving. Parallel parking. I can't turn around without aggravating my lower back. Then I get this visual aura like a migraine." I wave my hands in the air to illustrate the weird sparkly aura I get occasionally. I feel like I'm just rambling.

"And all this is from the Cushing's?" he asks.

"Yeah. It's kind of like a domino effect." I realize that the lawyer is just gathering info, but my thoughts are so scatterbrained I feel like I'm going on a stream of consciousness rant. One thing leads to another, then to another, and there seems to be no end in sight. This symptom causes this symptom causes this symptom. I am a collection of symptoms. To him, and now, to myself.

The lawyer sighs and puts down his pen. He gives me some documents to sign. He suggests applying for food stamps and worker's comp for my back.

"Thanks for walking up all those stairs," he says.

"No problem," I say, wondering if he says that to all his clients.

Bleeding

I PULL DOWN my underwear in a filthy bar bathroom and there it is on the crotch of my yellow, extra-large panties: blood, a dark crimson smear of it. I smile at the sight of my own blood. I haven't had my period in over a year. My period. My Aunt Flow.

In a family of six girls and a highly vocal mother, "our periods" are a constant source of conversation and complaint. And lately I've had nothing to add when the subject comes up. My menstruation, as irregular and inconsistent as it's been for the past decade, has now completely abandoned me. I feel as though I've lost an old friend. I can't say I miss the cramps and all the other baggage that goes along with a period, but I do feel left out. Less a woman. I wish my missing period wasn't just another a sign of my illness.

But there it is. Blood—plain as day on my underwear. I'm getting better, I tell myself. My hormone levels are finally getting back to normal. My old friend has returned.

I sit down on the toilet and have a little bit more watery diarrhea. I've been drinking way too much coffee the last couple of days and ever since I had my gall bladder out last fall, the diarrhea has been nearly constant. I've tried changing my diet but nothing seems to help. I do my business and pull up my underwear. I'm so happy to see the blood that I call my mom and one of my sisters and let them know I have blood on my underwear.

"That's fabulous, Martha!" says my mom.

But as the day progresses, I realize sheepishly that the blood is coming from the wrong place. It turns out my diarrhea has gotten so bad that I'm bleeding. So this is what my life has become, I think. Rectal bleeding.

I struggle through my beer and go home. I'm finally convinced to try the antidiarrheal medication my primary care doctor prescribed a couple weeks ago. I've been procrastinating on taking it mainly because the doctor said it might make me constipated. If there's anything I hate more than diarrhea, it's constipation. But rectal bleeding is the final straw. Never mind my period, I think, all I can imagine is my poor, puckered, irritated asshole. It's time for me to give the poor guy a break.

I go to my bedroom with a glass of water and open a packet of the cholestyramine antidiarrheal medication. The powder is "orange-flavored." I pour it into my glass and force myself to drink it down. The medication is slightly bitter, chalky and gritty. My stomach immediately starts making angry noises. It gurgles on and off for three hours.

At about 10:30 I go to bed and wait to fall asleep. Sometimes I pretend my insomnia is like a bear: if I lie still and play dead, it will wander off eventually. Not tonight. The bear doesn't leave me alone. There's an incredible amount of gas gurgling around in my intestines. Soon I find myself walking laps around the dark house farting loudly and repeatedly.

In the morning I drag myself out of bed and have diarrhea again.

Morning BM

WHEN I WAS a kid, probably eight or nine, I walked in on my grandpa while he was using the toilet.

More than the actual incident, what I remember is what my grandmother said to my mother afterwards. "Martha walked in on Jerry while he was having his morning BM!" she said, laughing.

To have the embarrassing incident recounted was one thing, but the whole concept of a "morning BM" horrified me. Was this what I had to look forward to as an adult, as an old person? Would I be on a delicate poop schedule, one that was to be protected, that bordered on the sacred? I decided that "No, that will NEVER happen to me."

But now, years later, like my grandpa, I am on my own poop schedule. My medication, in combination with the absence of my gall bladder, renders my digestive system a finicky master. I am a slave to its stubborn routine. Every morning, if I leave the house before having two or three bouts of diarrhea, I can guarantee that I will be running into a gas station or coffee shop and occupying their toilet for a good fifteen or twenty minutes.

So, like someone that my younger self would have scoffed at, been horrified by, I'm bound to a strict schedule, one that doesn't allow for spontaneity. I can't ignore this demanding body attached to my head.

My morning routine goes like this: shots and pills at 9:00; writing it all down along with my blood sugar levels in my drug log; coffee and cigarettes; and by 10:00 or 11:00, food of some kind. I've been doing this for over a year but I still haven't found a way to make it not suck. I usually turn on the radio to distract myself but sometimes it doesn't help. Sometimes I gag up my pills, sometimes I leak blood all over the place, sometimes I hurt myself and swear and break things. And somewhere in there, I try to take a dump.

Lately, I'm not even sure what I'm writing about, where this is all going. What is the purpose? I guess I've been flaking on a lot of people, canceling things at the last minute. I just want to let you know that I'm sorry and that it mostly has to do with poop.

THE GROVER

FAMILY MEETING

MINUTES

The Grover Family
Meeting Minutes

SOMNAMBULIST 15 was the distilled record of one year of my life: I had to move in with my parents and four of my seven siblings because of my health problems. Each week, on Sunday morning, we had a family meeting. I don't think I went one week without writing down what we talked about at the meetings. The result was this hilarious, weird, often-embarrassing zine.

In some ways, that year was the worst year of my life. I was really sick and had no money. But in other ways, it was the best year of my life. I don't know what I would have done without my family during that really difficult time. Although living with my parents, and living with a lot of people, period, was frustrating sometimes, they all loved me and helped me in ways that no roommates ever would or could.

Cast of Characters

LIVING IN THE HOUSE:

DAD: Mike Senior, electrician, sometimes assistant to Mom's real estate business.

MOM: Frani, Elsie, real estate agent, also working at a law firm to make ends meet.

SARAH: Older sister, nursing school student, working part-time at Tad's Chicken 'n Dumplings.

ME: Martha, Marty, etc. Working very part-time at an upscale grocery store. Mostly feeling crappy and watching daytime television.

RACHAEL: Rach, Mooker, etc. Younger sister. Working on a cruise ship on and off. Working at Tad's Chicken 'n Dumplings on and off.

MIKE JUNIOR: Mike, Mikey, "the boy," etc. Younger brother. Working on a cruise ship on and off. At Tad's on and off.

SIMONE: Younger sister. In high school. Working at Tad's.

NOT LIVING IN THE HOUSE (BUT MENTIONED PERIODICALLY):

ANA: Older sister, mother of three, married to Chad.

BEKAH: Adopted sister / friend, girlfriend to Hasan.

ZOE: Younger sister, one-time real estate agent.

WILL: Simone's boyfriend.

MAGGIE: Simone's friend.

September 7, 2008

1. Dad wants both his adult children (Sarah and I) to organize all our "storage items" in the garage.

2. I suggest starting a compost bin.

3. Sarah says we all need to start cleaning up the house more often.

4. I accuse someone in the family of taking my Ikea canister out of my bedroom and using it to prop open Sarah's bedroom window, causing it to bend. Dad says he was the one who put it in the window but that the canister was already in Sarah's room. No one will admit to taking it out of my room. Dad asks if there is any possibility that I was the one who left it in Sarah's room ... considering I had two brain surgeries this summer, considering I did sleep in Sarah's bedroom for my recovery.

I reply that that might be the case.

September 14, 2008

1. Mom brings up cigarette butts in the driveway, people drinking her very expensive Lactaid milk, and where are we going to put the greenhouse that Grandpa is getting rid of and where are we going to put the compost bin? The argument devolves into details involving the optimal combination of sunlight and swarms of flies and the minimal amount of wind and effort on everyone's part, including the flies. Nothing is resolved.

2. I bring up my "emotional needs."

"Could we just not refer to other people's stuff as crap or shit?" I say. "As in, will you please move your shit? "

We all laugh.

3. Dad asks us to sort the recycling appropriately and asks Sarah and me to label our stuff in the garage so he can move it with all the "Christmas crap."

I wag my finger at him.

"Oh, Christmas stuff, I mean," he says.

4. Sarah asks us to please put the cap back on the toothpaste and please put dishes in the left sink, please.

5. Simone and Mike have nothing to say.

6. After the meeting, Dad notices, for perhaps the first time, a ceramic statue of a woman with roses on top of the cupboard in the kitchen. The statue has been in the house, in various locations, for over a year. "What is this monstrosity?" he asks and picks it up. "We should just throw that away."

September 21, 2008

1. Sarah holds up a scratched pan and tells everyone to quit using "fucking forks" on the pans.

2. On the advice of my therapist, I suggest discontinuing the family meetings since they solve nothing and only raise false hopes.

3. Dad, Sarah, and Mom heartily defend the family meetings.

4. Simone and Mikey have nothing to add.

September 28, 2008

1. Dad asks us to put his computer to sleep at the end of the day and turn off the lights before we go to bed. He also notes that he's been doing a better job of putting the lid back on the recycling bin.

2. Mom asks for help next Saturday in the yard to get the compost bin moved.

3. Mike refuses to do his chores.

4. I suggest only half-heartedly that we all try to be more positive and that maybe we can institute some system of taxation on shoes left on the floor. Perhaps a quarter?

Mom doesn't think that's high enough. We should get charged a dollar for each pair of shoes. Sarah and Dad don't think it will work at all.

5. Simone has nothing to add.

October 5, 2008

1. Mom starts off the meeting by stating that she is having a nervous breakdown and to hide all the guns from her.

We all laugh.

2. Mom goes on to say that the compost bin has been moved and that we all need to start saving kitchen scraps. "But no protein," she says.

"Yeah, but you can compost almost anything," I say.

"I don't want any protein composted," she says.

"Why not? Because of pests, like raccoons or something?"

"No, because of maggots."

"How are maggots different than worms?"

"They're gross."

"Will not putting protein in the compost solve the maggot problem?" Dad asks.

"I don't know," Mom answers. "Also—I need help putting the greenhouse up."
Dad looks at Mikey.

Mom looks at Mikey. "I would also like the lawn mowed."

"You can compost almost anything," I say.

"That's already been established," Dad says.

"It's raining pretty hard today," Mikey says.

"Martha is having a party next Monday and I would like that lawn mowed."

Mikey sighs and lays sideways on the couch. "There is nothing I like worse than mowing wet grass."

"Name three things that you like better than mowing wet grass but not as much as you like mowing dry grass," Dad says.

This question confuses Mikey.

3. I tell Mom and Dad that I unloaded and loaded the dishwasher twice yesterday and that to please rinse their dishes and put them on the left side of the sink.

4. Several other things are said and Sarah starts to cry.

5. Simone comes home and sits down.

6. Zoe calls and we put her on speakerphone. Zoe is bored and alone at a real estate open house. "What's going on?" she asks.

"Oh, nothing. Just having a family meeting," we say.

"How's it going?"

"Oh, same as always."

October 12, 2008

1. Dad and I come in from the TV room at Sarah's bidding. I'm wrapped in a down comforter and I lay down on the couch.

2. Dad sits on the other couch and props his feet up on the coffee table and comments on how long his toenails are. "I could cut those toenails with a lawnmower," he says.

3. I ask that everyone rinse their dishes and set them on the left-hand side of the sink. I also ask that we all try to keep the lid on the compost bin to ward off fruit flies.

4. Sarah and Mom fold laundry while Dad and I stare off into space.

5. Sarah tells Dad that she and her friend Jacob will be moving the green bookshelf into the garage. Sarah and Dad get into an argument about the bookshelf. Dad tells Sarah that he loves her and he loves all his children. Sarah tells Dad that she knows that he loves her but that he talks to her like she is an idiot. Dad tells Sarah that he knows she's not an idiot.

"Did you ever think maybe I'm just crazy?" he says.

Sarah tells Dad that she's thought of that, but that's no excuse.

6. Simone has nothing to add.

October 19, 2008

1. Everyone is very tired this morning. Mom reclines on the couch and says she needs her medication to get off the couch but that she can't get off the couch without her medication.

2. I sit by the end table and eat some double fudge Mother's cookies.

3. Sarah asks everyone what we thought of her new boyfriend Jacob. We all think he was nice. I wonder if he thought I was weird because of all the Jew jokes I was making. He didn't.

4. Mom asks how we are doing in the kitchen. Everyone thinks we are doing pretty good.

5. I tell Simone to remember to close the shower curtain and throw the towel over the rod when she is done showering. She says she will try to remember.

6. I say that we are fast filling up the compost bin. Mom says that we need to stir it.

7. I say that if I don't go to grad school next year, I want to start a garden.

8. Dad asks Simone if she has anything to add.

"I think the family meeting is over," she says.

October 26, 2008

1. I'm so tired this morning I have to be practically drug out of bed.

2. Sarah and Mom get into an argument about the fact that we don't have a coffee maker.

"I need to find a coffee maker with a conical filter," Mom says.

"They make coffee makers like that," Sarah says.

"I know, but they're very expensive," Mom says.

"I bet if you guys abstained from ice cream for a month you could afford one," says Sarah.

"Ooh, hitting below the belt," says Dad.

3. I tell everyone that last night during one of my insomniac walks I found the front door of the house blown open. The wind was heavy last night. Leaves were blowing into the house.

4. Simone says she slept with three blankets and a hat and wool socks.

5. I tell Mom and Dad that I would like to help them with yard work but that I can't lift anything because the doctor told me I could get a hernia.

"We don't want you to get a hernia," Dad says.

"Well, I'm only telling you because the canopy blew over last week and I can't help you take it apart."

"Oh crap! I totally forgot about that. Thanks for reminding me," says Dad.

November 2, 2008

1. As we are gathering together in the living room, Mom tells us about Beverly Cleary's childhood. (She is reading Beverly Cleary's autobiography.)

"Beverly Cleary had braces for six years!" she says. "After five years of braces her orthodontist decided she had too many teeth and pulled some of them, then put the braces back on."

"Sounds like he wasn't a very good orthodontist," Dad says.

2. Dad says that we are all doing a good job of keeping the back door locked so it won't blow open during the night. Mom comments that there hasn't really been any wind lately.

3. I ask Dad if he's called Uncle Mitch about the table in the backyard.

Dad answers that no he hasn't, but he did buy a tarp and covered the glass table with it.

"Was the table already damaged?" I ask.

"Well, yes."

"So, Martha and I were right—that it would get damaged outside." Sarah says with a smile.

With some hesitation Dad admits that yes, we were right.

"I just can't believe that you guys would put that table outside—but I figured—hey, it's your house, you can do what you want," says Sarah.

"Well, thank you for admitting that yes, it is our house," says Mom.

4. There is a moment of silence.

5. "Does Will (Simone's boyfriend) think we hate him?" asks Sarah.

Simone nods.

"We don't hate Will," says Mom.

"Next time he comes over I'll tell him how much we like him," says Dad.

"No, then he'll just think you're being sarcastic," says Simone.

"You know," Mom says, "really it's better for your parents to hate your boyfriend than to really like him and pressure you to stay with him even if he's not a good match for you. That's what Beverly Cleary's mom did. Beverly Cleary was an only child. I would have been a horrible mother to just one child."

November 9, 2008

1. Simone and Mom are the only ones who didn't cry today in the family meeting.

November 16, 2008

1. Dad lays down the rules for Simone going over to her boyfriend, Will's, house:

A. She must have all her homework done.

B. His parents must be home.

C. It must be at a reasonable hour.

D. And next time they see each other, he must come over to our house.

E. AND she has to ask.

2. I wonder why the meeting started so early.

"We always start at 9:00," Mom says.

"I thought we were gonna start at 9:30."

"Nope," says Sarah. "You were the one that wanted to start earlier."

"I was?"

"Yeah."

3. Mom and Sarah go over the menu for Thanksgiving. (I'm in charge of getting a free-range turkey. The biggest one I can get. Also, the fruit salad so that Mom or Grandma won't put yogurt on it.)

Turkey – Mom

Stuffing – Mom

Gravy – Mom

Potatoes – Mom

Pies – Sarah

Bread – Grandma

Yams – Ana

Soda – Simone

November 23, 2008

It's 9:45 and Dad knocks on my door. "Your mom and Sarah want to start the family meeting."

1. I limp into the living room.

2. Mom can't find her ADD medication.

We finally decide that it must be in her car and start the meeting.

3. The subject of Thanksgiving is brought up. The menu has been adjusted. I am no longer in charge of anything. Zoe's German friend Steven is no longer attending and Sarah's friend Andy from nursing school is.

4. "How are we going to get the house in order before Thursday?" Sarah wants to know.

"Yes, we need to talk about that," says Mom.

"All I can say is that I can barely move because my back is fucked up," I say. "I can unload the top of the dishwasher but not the bottom. I can sit in a chair and unload the bottom."

"I'll unload the bottom," Dad says.

"Are you really going to do that? Or are you just saying that?" I ask. "Because it seems like every time I ask you to do that you act like I'm putting you out or you pawn it off on Simone."

Dad sighs. "I will try and act like I want to do it."

5. Mom puts her hand up. "Can I say something? I read this book once—it was called *Men are from Mars, Women are from Venus*. It helped me so much. In the book it talked about how when you ask a man to do something he will always act like he doesn't want to do it, but unless he explicitly says 'no' he'll do it. But men have their whole day planned out and even if it looks like they're not doing anything, if it looks like they're just staring at the wall, they see your request as an interruption."

I tell Mom that I appreciate her input but don't know it if it's applicable.

6. Mom brings up the fact that no one has been sweeping the kitchen floor. She suggests that she will take over sweeping as her chore in exchange for not doing the dishes.

Neither Sarah nor myself think that's a fair trade.

November 30, 2008

(Simone is in San Francisco. Rachael has moved in temporarily and is sharing Simone's room.)

1. I have to be drug out of bed this morning.

2. Dad's first item on the list is the dishwasher and its constant leaking.

Mom doesn't think we'll be able to afford a new seal for the dishwasher for another six months.

3. Dad's second item of business is installing an outdoor light in front of the house. Sarah's stereo was stolen out of her car the night before Thanksgiving. The car was parked in our driveway.

We all agree that's a good idea.

"Man, and I had just read that article about things you can do to keep your car from being broken into," says Sarah, and takes another drink of her coffee. "And I didn't do any of them!"

"What did the article say?" asks Dad.

"Well first of all, to lock your car!"

"What else did it say?"

"They said the best thing you can do is to keep your car clean. Don't have change lying around. Dad, the other day when I borrowed your truck, there was three bucks on the dash. I put it in your glove box."

Dad looks around at all of us. "We're all going to start keeping our cars clean." I laugh. "I'll try."

"Well, do you want your stereo stolen?" Dad asks.

"I have a tape player," I say. "No one is stealing my stereo."

4. I tell Rachael that she needs to get the towel system in the bathroom figured out.

"What do you mean?" she wants to know.

"You close the curtain," Sarah makes a sweeping motion with one hand "and then you throw the ground towel over the rod. Don't put your personal towel over the curtain rod."

"Oh—I wasn't aware that was the system," says Rachael.

"Well, now you know," I say.

December 7, 2008

(Rachael is in Seattle. Simone is back from San Francisco.)

1. As usual, I'm very tired this morning and am the last one up.

2. From my bed, I ask Simone to ask Sarah to make a full pot of coffee so everyone can share.

"She's already doing that," Simone says.

3. I get out of bed and sit down on the couch.

The tea kettle starts to whistle and Mom runs on her tippy toes into the kitchen. "I can barely walk, but I'll get that," she says.

"What's wrong with you?" I ask.

"She rubbed all the skin off her heels with a nail file," says Sarah. "Just imagine if she were a drug addict!" Sarah is knitting furiously on the couch.

Mom sits back down on the couch. "As long as no one steps on my heels or kicks my heels, I think I'll be fine," she says.

4. "Can we start the meeting?" Sarah asks.

5. Dad puts his hands together. "So where are you going today, Simone?"

"To Will's Grandma's house."

"Where does she live?"

"I don't know."

"I don't understand why it's such a big deal to go to Will's Grandma's house."

"Cause she lives far away. Like an hour away and they don't get to see her that often. Plus I'm excited because she has a puppy."

"Where does she live?" Mom asks.

"I don't know," says Simone.

"Can we start the meeting?" asks Sarah.

"Yeah," I say. "I have nothing to add. I feel really sick."

"You better not come home with a puppy," says Dad.

6. "Dad, can you fix the clothes dryer in the other bathroom today? If you need help, I'll help you," says Sarah.

"He tried to fix it last week but the washer was full of water and he couldn't move it," Mom says.

"I tried to fix it last week," Dad says.

"Well, there aren't any clothes in there now so you can do it right after the meeting," says Sarah.

"There actually might be some clothes in there right now," says Mom.

Sarah wants to know why anyone is doing laundry in that bathroom anyway.

7. I wonder if I can take a shower. I feel very sick.

8. Sarah concludes the meeting by asking me to stop monopolizing the table in the TV room with all my crap.

"I'll try and remember to clear it off," I say.

9. "Wait, lets talk about the Christmas tree," Mom says.

"Put it wherever you want," says Sarah.

"Where do you think I should put it?" Mom asks Dad.

"I'm neutral," Dad says.

"You don't have an opinion?"

"Put it right there," Dad says and points.

"Then where will I put the table?" Mom wants to know.

"Move that table over there," Dad says and points behind him.

"Mom, just put it where we normally put it," says Sarah.

10. I get up and get in the shower.

December 14, 2008

(Rachael is MIA)

1. I am up surprisingly early and am able to start the meeting without having to be drug out of bed.

2. To begin, Dad asks me to re-introduce the idea I had brought up last night while we were watching *America's Funniest Home Videos*.

"I think we should change the day and the time of the family meeting," I say. "I don't like having it on Sunday mornings because first of all, personally, I feel the sickest on Sunday mornings. I'm tired from having just worked two days, and I get sick after I take my medication. Also people have whined about having to get up on Sunday morning and if I had a social life I might complain about that too. Also, when we talk about chores we want Dad to do, it just seems like he would have a better time remembering if the meeting were to come before his weekend rather than at the tail end of it."

Sarah says that there is no way because of her schedule in nursing school that she could accommodate a change in the time of the meeting.

Dad says that the only other time that he could see the meeting working would be on Saturday morning.

Mom says she would be willing to change it to Sunday night.

"Changing the meeting time won't help Dad remember anything," says Sarah.

3. "I think we should require Rachael to come to the meetings," says Sarah.

"I agree," I say. "Her stuff is here, she needs to come to the meetings. It's not fair that she isn't here."

"We need to make Simone and Rachael a better situation than that room," says Mom.

Sarah states that she has offered four times to help Rachael and Simone move Mikey's shit down to the garage to make room for their shit.

I suggest that they obviously don't care.

4. I say that I unloaded and loaded the dishwasher last night and that I refuse to do any more dishes because I wasn't even here on Saturday to eat the big breakfast that Zoe cooked for her German friend Steven, so I wasn't going to do the pans.

"I'll do it," says Mom. "And I would've done it last night, too, but I would rather have talked to you. And like this morning, I'd just rather be with my family than do dishes. If the kitchen were next to the TV it would be spotless!"

"Like your office, right Mom?" I say.

Sarah and I laugh.

"Burn!" says Sarah.

Mom says that we hurt her feelings. "That's the second time you've laughed at me this morning. My disorganization is a sore spot for me," she says.

I apologize for making fun of her.

5. Dad adds that we need to remember to lock the door at night and turn off all the lights.

6. Sarah tells Simone that the bathroom is disgusting and that she and Rachael need to clean it.

7. We ask Simone how the Christmas party at her boyfriend Will's house was last night.

"It was fun," she says.

Sarah asks Simone how her meeting went with Judy, her boss.

"It was fine," she says.

Mom asks Simone if she knows where the SAT books are that Mom gave her. Simone says she does. "We should do that today," Mom says.

8. "How do you drive in the snow?" Simone wants to know.

"You don't," say Mom and Sarah.

"Then how will I see Will?" asks Simone.

"It's his turn to come over here," says Dad. "You do understand that rule—don't you, Simone?"

"Why are you trying to control our relationship?" asks Simone. "I have to know how to drive in the snow because his car is stuck in the ditch at his house. I have to go pick him up."

"He has to get his own car out of the ditch," Dad says.

"It'll be good for him," says Sarah.

"Men like a challenge," says Mom.

December 21, 2008

(Simone is snowed in over at her friend Maggie's house)

1. Sarah wants to know what the status is on the razors in the shower.

I say I must have some new ones somewhere.

"Well, we shouldn't be sharing razors. It's disgusting and unhygienic."

"I agree," I say.

2. "That shower is disgusting," I say. "I think Rachael and Simone should clean it."

"I am not cleaning it myself," says Rachael. "I also am not cleaning that room myself. That would just be a continuation of the pattern between us since we were kids. Where Simone does nothing and I have to do everything."

3. Mom says that she noticed that no one has been rinsing their dishes. She loaded the dishwasher last night and came across a full bowl of noodles that hadn't been rinsed. "I think it was yours, Martha," she says.

"I didn't eat pasta yesterday," I say. "It was Simone's."

4. Dad asks us to please turn off the lights in our bedrooms when we leave them.

5. Dad informs Rachael that she is expected to come to the family meetings if she is staying with us.

6. Mom gets up and checks the water level in the Christmas tree stand. "Jeez, that thing is already dry," she says.

"That has got to be the driest Christmas tree we've ever had," says Dad. "Look at all those needles on the ground."

"Well, it passed the dry test at the lot," says Mom.

"What dry test?" Dad wants to know.

"You run your fingers along a branch, and if needles come off, the tree is too dry. No needles came off, so," Mom shrugs.

"That's a bullshit test," says Dad.

December 28, 2008

(Sarah is in Mexico. Simone has spent the night at her friend Maggie's house.)

1. It's 9:15 a.m. and Simone is not home yet. While we wait for her to arrive, Mom tells us about her dream last night. Rachael moans from the couch that she is going back to bed until Simone gets home. Dad tells us about the stupid detective show he watched last night.

"What was it about?" I ask.

"It's so stupid I'd be embarrassed to describe it to you," says Dad. He goes on to describe the plot.

I remember what I dreamt last night and tell everyone all about it.

Rachael calls Simone on her cell phone. "She's on her way," she says.

2. Simone and Maggie walk in and sit down. It's 10:00. I tell Maggie she has to sit in on our family meeting because she made Simone late.

"Why were you late?" asks Dad.

"You should thank me," says Maggie. "This morning we got caught by the police selling meth and I talked them into letting Simone and I free."

"Oh really?" we say.

3. "I have three issues," I say. "Two of them are for Simone and Rachael and one is for everyone. So—Simone and Rachael? I'd appreciate it if you wouldn't throw your jackets and scarves on the family room floor. If you are going to throw them on the floor, throw them on the floor of your room."

"Okay," they say.

"I also want one of you or both of you to clean that bathroom before Sarah gets home," I say.

"I scrubbed the floor, toilet, and sink on Christmas Eve," says Rachael. "So I think that Simone should do the shower."

"I don't care who does it, I just think it should get done before Sarah gets home. Oh yeah, I have four things actually—Simone, is that all your junk in the hallway bathroom? Could you clean that up?"

Simone nods.

Maggie answers her phone. "I have to go," she says. "My mom needs the car."

4. "We spend way too much on food," I go on. "And we throw way too much away. We should all try to eat what we have here instead of constantly buying more food."

Dad says he couldn't agree more, but that sometimes if he doesn't see a can of peaches in the first row in the cupboard, he just assumes we don't have any.

Rachael says that she doesn't always know what's in the fridge and that she doesn't know what's in "all those containers."

5. "By the way," I say. "Mom, did you want us to start paying you money for bills?"

Dad points out that he doesn't know what my budget is. I answer that I can't afford more than about $50 a month. Mom says that she was thinking about charging us all for one bill.

Simone asks if she is going to be charged, too. "I haven't worked in over a month," she says.

"No, you're still in high school. You have to obey us."

"So, you realize that if Simone pays you then she is an adult and you have to treat her like an adult?" asks Rachael.

Mom points out that most children struggle with living under their parent's house and rules when they're over eighteen.

Simone points out that if they would treat her like she was eighteen and not twelve she might not struggle.

6. Mom laughs and says her next point is the opposite of my last point. "I had some granola and some gross, healthy cereal in the cupboard and I mixed them

together because it was the only way to get myself to eat the healthy cereal. But the other day I went to mix them together and there was no more granola."

"That was me," I say.

"Well anyway, my point is that if you eat all my granola, buy some more."

"Okay. But how is that the opposite of my point?"

"Because it's about buying more food."

"Oh."

7. Mom asks if anyone else has anything to add. No one does.

January 4, 2009

(Sarah is back from Mexico. Rachael is MIA.)

1. I'm so tired I lay on the floor using the beanbag chair as a pillow.

2. Mom goes over her schedule and informs Dad that they've been invited to an epiphany party at their friend's house on Tuesday.

"What's an epiphany party?" I ask.

"It's something to do with the three wise men."

"I've had an epiphany that I don't like to go out on weeknights," Dad says.

3. Mom suggests we all try to keep each other involved in shopping so that we don't spend extra money on food.

Dad says that he's been cooking himself more meals because Mom has been working late. "Like the other day, I cooked myself some mini-steaks," he says. "But you came home and they were still frozen in the pan," he says to Mom.

"Yeah, I came home and turned up the burner for you," Mom says.

"But I *can* cook for myself," says Dad.

4. Dad says he has some minor points: turn off the lights when you leave the room and lock the back door at night.

5. Mom says that she had a very satisfying conversation with Simone and her boyfriend Will.

I ask if we really have to talk about this at the family meeting.

Dad apologizes and pats me on the thigh.

6. I ask if I can get up and take my medication if we don't have anything else to talk about.

January 11, 2009

(Rachael is MIA again.)

1. Mom comes out of her bedroom in her bathrobe and sits down in front of the fireplace and closes her eyes. "Where's the coffee?" she asks.

"I piggybacked on Martha's cup," says Dad. "I used her grounds. I hitched a cup as they say in the railroad business."

"Well, can I be the caboose?" asks Mom.

"Sure," says Dad and goes into the kitchen to start the coffee.

2. "Rachael isn't here again," I say. "What's the consequence for this?"

Mom thinks she should have to do the dishes for a week.

I think a week is a long time.

Dad says she should come home and clean the whole house. Mom gets up and starts folding the laundry. "Yes, but what does 'clean the house' mean? That means different things to different people."

"We should take a vote," says Dad. He raises his hand. "I think Rachael should come home today and clean the whole house."

Sarah and I disagree. Sarah thinks Rachael should come home and clean the fridge or the bathroom.

"That doesn't seem like that big of a deal to me," says Dad. "That doesn't seem like that big of a job."

"Oh yes it is," says Mom.

"That bathroom is disgusting," says Sarah. "She needs to detail the bathroom. Detail. Scrub the floor."

"Did anyone tell Rachael she needs to be at these meetings after she missed the last one?" I ask.

"Oh yeah! I told Rachael that she needed to come to the meetings," says Dad.

"Yeah, but did you tell her what would happen if she didn't?"

"Well, I don't like to make threats," says Dad.

"It's not about threats, Dad, it's about boundaries. She needs to know where the boundaries are," says Sarah. "I don't think it's fair for her to come home to this irrational reaction."

"Thanks Sarah," says Dad. "I appreciate that. Sometimes I need people to tell me when I'm being irrational—that's how irrational I am."

We all agree that Rachael needs to come home and clean the bathroom.

"Detail," says Sarah.

3. Mom says that she has several clients that are on the "precipice" of listing their houses with her.

"So you're gonna be busy next week," Sarah says.

"Yep. And they have more work they want me to do at the firm," says Mom. She goes into the kitchen and makes herself coffee.

4. "I have several minor issues," says Dad, looking down at his post-it notes. "It seems to me that the compost people may need to rethink the compost ... "

Blame is shuttled around about the overflowing compost bin. We all agree to take it out more often.

5. "Okay, and Rachael said she would pay $50 a month as rent," says Dad. "She volunteered to pay! We didn't ask her. I think it's her way of assuaging her guilt."

"When did she say that?" I ask. "I thought we were all going to split up a bill."

"She said that at the last meeting," says Dad.

"You're misremembering that," I say. "She wasn't here at the last meeting. I thought we were going to split up a bill. The gas bill. I can't afford to pay more than $50 a month. Mom brought it up and said we would talk about it when everyone was here."

"And now we're all not here again," says Sarah.

"I want you four to split up the gas bill," says Mom.

"I'm in high school," says Simone. "I haven't worked in two months."

"Frani, Simone doesn't have to pay," says Dad.

"Okay, well the three adults, who are basically unemployed, will pay the gas bill," says Mom.

"I'll be in charge of that," says Sarah. "You give me the bill and I'll make sure it's paid. I'll be in charge of collecting the money."

6. Simone spreads out her arms to everyone. "Okay, everyone," she says. Simone says that she and her boyfriend Will are starting on a new health regimen. They're going to start working out together. "So that means I probably won't be able to make it home by 6:00 pm."

"Will is gonna have to start eating," says Sarah.

"I know. He said that when he works out he gets really hungry."

"Alright, but I don't want this to turn into you taking Will home. He needs to drive his own car home," says Dad.

"Okay," says Simone.

"And you need to come home first."

"Why?" asks Simone. "I'll go over to Will's, we'll eat lunch, and then we'll go swimming."

"Eat lunch? You eat lunch at 4:00 p.m.?"

"Yes!" says Simone.

"I don't know what to say to you, Simone," says Dad. "I'm blank and vacuous."

"Like Keanu Reeves," I say.

Dad laughs. "Yes, like Keanu Reeves."

January 18, 2009
(Rachael is in Mexico. Sarah is in Seattle.)

1. "Simone, if I tell you something, will you promise not to tell Maggie?" asks Mom.

"What?" says Simone.

"Last night when your dad and I saw that James Bond movie, I kept thinking every time I saw his face that he looked just like Maggie."

"You know, that actor also looks just like that creepy guy from *Amelie* that sits at the bar and harasses everybody," says Dad.

"The heavy brow," I say.

"Yes, the heavy brow," says Mom.

2. Both couches in the living room are covered with laundry. Mom is folding it. Simone and I sit on the ground and drink our coffee. Simone and Mom argue about the laundry: whether Mom and Dad might have a problem with putting their laundry in their room.

Mom says it will never happen.

3. "Okay! Dad, what do you have to say today?" I ask.

"I have two minor points," Dad says. "Please remember to close the outside gates when you open them, and a couple nights ago I found the back door open."

4. All the needles on the Christmas tree in the front yard have blown off. The empty aquarium in the front yard is full of frozen water. Mom pauses in front of the window. "We need to get those two things cleaned up today," she says to Dad.

5. "Do you have anything to add, Mom?" I ask.

"Yes. I realize that we've been letting things slip around here lately. And by 'we' I mean 'me.' I need to get all these nativity sets put away."

Mom and Dad discuss the nativity sets and boxes in the garage. I tell her that I will help put them away in the next couple days because my friend Maria is coming over for dinner on Wednesday.

"I also want you to know that you're all welcome to accompany me to church on Sunday," Mom says.

6. Ana calls and we ask her if she has anything to add to the family meeting.

Mom hangs up the phone. "She's coming over with Chad and the kids. Their power is out and they have no hot water."

7. "All right!" I say. "I have some issues!"

"Well, we didn't know you've been waiting," says Mom.

"Go ahead Martha," says Dad.

"The kitchen floor is basically being destroyed right now because of the leaking dishwasher. I talked to Dad about maybe hand-washing the dishes and he wasn't too hot on that idea. So I was thinking maybe we could do our basic dishes by hand and use the dishwasher for just the pots and pans."

"We need to get on the Internet today and order that part. That seal for the dishwasher," says Mom. "That floor is ruined. And it's rotting. We're gonna have dry rot."

8. "Frani, didn't the gas bill come in the mail?" asks Dad.

"Yes it did."

"Well, give it to Sarah. And she's going to give it to the three people with money in the house."

"Well now Rachael is not here."

"Yeah," says Dad. "And the whole reason we got this whole thing going was trying to get some kind of money out of Rachael." Dad looks out the window. "You know, the other day I was thinking about how nice it would be to ask Mike to mow the lawn. Now he's not here and there is no buffer between me and the chores!"

Dad goes on to list the chores he had to do when he was a kid. "We had to feed the chickens. We had to feed the cows two bales of hay every morning. We had to feed the dogs and the pigs. And the girls, the girls kept the house and prepared all the meals. There was no question. We fed the cows in December and we fed them in January. If we didn't feed them, then no one else would. We fed them every morning. In March, in April. There was no question, that was just the way it was."

Mom starts matching the socks. "That wasn't the way I was raised. There was no consistency in my house. I was put in charge of feeding a rabbit when I was a kid and the rabbit died. I've always felt horrible about that.

'You know, I don't have the personality to have a big family. I just don't! I'm a party girl. I mean I could get you all to the park and we could have a picnic ...

'Other people get up in the morning and think about what they have to do that day. I don't think about those things. I just don't. I'm thinking about other things."

"Well, you just need to try harder, Mom," I say.

Mom and I laugh.

9. "I have other things to add!" I say. " I want to have a Valentines'-making party here. What day would be good for you guys?"

"I don't care," says Dad. We decide on February 10.

10. "Also Dad, would you please clean off your desk?" I say.

Dad sighs. "Yes, but that is low on my priority list."

"Well, I want to clean the TV room and I don't want to clean your desk because I don't know where any of that stuff goes."

"I don't want you to clean it off either but I have a lot of other stuff to do today."

"You don't have to do it today, just do it before my Valentines' party."

"Okay."

"Martha," Mom says, "in the 30 years I've been married to your father I've asked him to clean off his desk many times and guess who ends up cleaning it? Me."

"So you don't mind other people cleaning off your desk?" I ask.

"I do mind," says Dad. "Just remind me every four days or so and I'll do it. That seems to be the way things work around here," says Dad, and walks out of the room.

"It's not that hard, Dad," I say. "Just throw it in a box."

11. The power goes off.

January 25, 2009

(I'm at the beach—Mom wrote the minutes.)

9:30 a.m. Simone is not yet home. It snowed last night.

9:55 a.m. Simone makes it home from spending the night at Maggie's.

Just as we sit down, Zoe calls Simone's phone to say she's on her way over to start breakfast.

I notice the Christmas decorations not yet entirely put away—the pile of laundry on the loveseat.

I speak up first. I remind everyone to use the front door due to the snow.

Mike responds with, "I'm not going out all day today."

Mike mentions the back door needs to be shut tight. He found it open again.

Sarah complains that when she got home the other night, Mike and I had left all the lights on when we went out.

Simone pipes up that the house is so cold she has to sleep with four fluffy blankets, a down comforter, and a heating pad.

I comment it was 61 degrees in the house when I got up. I turned it up to 65. Sarah said she's keeping a close watch on the thermostat since she's the one paying the bill.

I tell everyone I'm going to get as many hours in at the firm as possible in the next two weeks to earn the balance needed to pay the mortgage.

Sarah tells us she's going to be two nights a week working swing for her schooling.

Simone expresses needing help with applying for college.

Sarah reports her car is running better and tells us about the conversation she had with Steve, her mechanic / friend. He told her he was going to get her car running so well she'd wash it more often. Sarah said, "Like my Mom." Steve, glancing at my car, replied, "Your mom doesn't keep her car clean."

Mike says he's planning to get a faucet set up on the driveway but his sump pump uses the hole in the garage cement wall currently and he'll have to solve that obstacle.

Zoe walks in with her arms full of groceries.

Meeting is disbanded.

February 1, 2009

1. Dad comes out of his bedroom in a button-up dress shirt and flannel pajama bottoms. "I was having the most vivid dream. It sucks to be woken up from a vivid dream." He sits down on the beanbag chair by the fireplace.

"Did you wear that shirt to bed?" I ask.

Dad looks down at his shirt. "Yes. It was very comfortable. I was watching *Zoolander* last night and he was wearing these exact same pajamas."

"Blue pajamas with penguins on them?" asks Mom. "That's hysterical!"

"Yes, but his was a one-piece."

2. Mom is folding the laundry. "When I leave for Mexico next week, Mike, I

want you to carry your phone with you at all times, so you and Simone can stay in contact."

"Okay, but I'm not going to take it with me to work. I'm going to leave it in my truck. Besides, you won't be able to call me from Mexico, anyway."

"I know, but I want you two," she points at Simone and Dad, "to stay in better contact."

"I have no problem keeping in contact," Simone says, and throws up her hands.

3. Dad tells everyone to remember to turn off their space heaters before they leave the house.

4. Sarah says that she is the only one who ever turns off the lights.

"At night?" I ask.

"No, before they leave the house. Mom, you NEVER turn off your office lights."

"There is a reason for that," says Mom. "I think it makes the house look like there is someone here if the light is on."

5. Dad rubs his face. "Man, I was having the most vivid dream."

6. "I have several things to add," I say. "Mom, this pertains to you because I already talked to Sarah and Dad about this. We have way too much rotting food in the salad drawers in the fridge. So you either need to look before you go shopping, or throw rotting stuff away when you get home instead of just shoving it on top of the old stuff."

Mom nods.

7. I also let Simone know that she needs to pull her car further into her parking spot because yesterday I nearly hit her car when I was backing out.

8. Mom starts talking about her trip to Mexico next week.

9. "Do you have anything else to add, Dad?" Sarah asks.

Dad shakes his head. "I was having the most vivid dream," he says.

"We know!" I say. "You've said that like five times."

Dad points at Sarah, "Well, I know you don't want to hear about my dream."

"You're right. Thank you," she says.

"Well, it wasn't so much what it was about. It was just so vivid—that made it good."

"Except if it's a nightmare," I say.

"Sarah, when you were gone, we all sat around and told each other our dreams," says Mom.

"That's right!" I say. Mom and I laugh.

10. Zoe walks in in her workout clothes with a banana.

"Zoe!" we all say.

"Oh," she says. "I forgot it was the family meeting." She sits down on the hearth and starts eating her banana.

11. Zoe, Mom, and Dad start talking about taxes.

12. Sarah and Simone get up and leave.

13. "Is the meeting over?" I ask.

14. Mom and Zoe and Dad ignore me.

15. "I have one more thing to add," I say. "Dad—this is your second warning to clean off your desk."

February 8, 2009

(Simone is house-sitting for Will's parents.)

1. Sarah comes out of her bedroom and asks if the meeting has started yet.

"The coffee is still brewing," I say. "Let's wait until it's ready."

"I thought the meetings start at 9:00."

"They start at 9:30," says Dad.

2. Sarah asks me how work was.

"Crappy. I had another blood sugar crash and went home early."

Sarah asks me what I had for breakfast.

"Pound-cake and an apple."

"You can't eat that way. You need protein in the morning."

"I know, but it just comes on so quickly. Someone I work with said that I need to do something before that happens."

"Well he's right!" says Mom. "I have blood sugar crashes all the time and I'm not up walking around like you at your job. When you're fucking working you need to eat a substantial breakfast!"

"Martha, it's hard to sit here and listen to you do the same thing over and over," says Sarah.

"I don't feel like I am doing the same thing over and over."

"You are," says Dad.

"You see?" says Mom. "They agree with me! And I was just gonna sit here and keep my mouth shut. But I had to open my mouth and pull out the big guns! With the 'f' word!"

"You used the 'f' word?" I ask.

"Yeah."

"Oh, I didn't notice."

3. "We need to stay on track," says Sarah. "I have to make a cake for Ana."

4. "I'm asking Dad again to clean off the desk before my party on Wednesday," I say.

5. "I know you have to make a cake," Dad says, and points at Sarah. "But I just have to say I was watching the news last night and they showed these people taking a dog into the grocery store and the dog was running around the store off the leash and the dog stole a bone off the shelf and ran out of the store with it!"

6. I ask Mom to stop leaving the half and half on the counter in the morning.

This conversation continues until Dad is threatening to follow Mom around and observe her morning routine.

7. Simone walks in and sits down. "You started the meeting without me?"

"The meeting starts at 9:00," says Sarah.

"I thought it starts at 9:30," says Simone.

"We never really decided," I say.

"Who wants it at 9:30?" asks Simone.

Everyone raises their hand except Sarah.

"Ha ha! You're out-voted!" says Simone.

8. Dad says he only has a minor issue—that there is something wrong with the thermostat and that he wants it turned down when we're all gone.

9. "How's house-sitting at Will's house?" Mom asks.

"It's nice to have some alone time," says Simone. "Will and his Dad asked me not to have Maggie over."

February 15, 2009

1. There is a pile of assorted canned goods on the coffee table: canned cherries, about five cans of evaporated milk, bread crumbs, fish sauce, and clam chowder.

"What's this?" I ask.

"That's Dad's deal," says Sarah.

"Okay," says Dad. "I'm not saying there isn't room for your food, or your food, or your food in the cupboard." He points at each of us. "What I AM saying, is that there isn't enough room for any of our food AND this stuff in the cupboard."

"Do you know what I use this for?" Sarah picks up a can of evaporated milk.

"No. What?"

"Pecan pie, Mike," says Mom.

"Well, do we really need five cans of it?" asks Dad.

Sarah throws up her hands. "I don't really care, but I'm just saying that I might not make it if it wasn't in the cupboard."

"You wouldn't make pie?" asks Dad.

"Maybe, but really this is an issue between you and Mom. I couldn't care less."

"Yeah, I don't care either," I say.

"Look, I'm not trying to make anyone defensive here. I just don't see why we need five cans of evaporated milk," says Dad.

"Then what are you saying?" asks Sarah.

Dad picks up a jar of fish sauce. "I'm just trying to give you an opportunity to say, 'Yeah, we don't need all this food!'"

"So you're giving us an opportunity to agree with you?" I ask.

"Exactly," says Dad.

"We both agree with you, Dad. We don't care. Get rid of it," says Sarah.

"Yeah," I say. "Get rid of it. Don't leave it on the coffee table."

"Yeah," says Sarah. "You've made your point, now get rid of it. Take responsibility for this stuff. Don't just leave it here."

2. Simone asks if she and Will can go somewhere for spring break.

"You and Will alone together?" asks Dad.

"Well, maybe someone else will go with us," says Simone.

"You and Will together? No. Absolutely not," says Dad. "I'm gonna say that right now. No way."

"What!?" says Simone. "Well, can I go with his family to Hawaii this summer?"

"With his family? Yes," says Dad. "Absolutely."

"That's awesome, Simone!" I say.

3. Mom waves a piece of paper and sets it down on the foot rest. "Did everyone see this list? This is my rebuttal, or, well, my response to last week's meeting. This is a list of adult ADHD traits and symptoms. And let me tell you, I have every single one of these symptoms. Every single one."

"I saw it, Mom," says Sarah.

I tell Mom she needs a life coach. She replies that she can't afford one. I tell her that I will be her life coach. I remind her that she told us that people with ADHD need someone following them around keeping them on track.

"I will do that," I say. "You told us that you leave things out because you don't notice. Well, instead of just hoping that you will notice, I'm gonna start saying something."

"Thanks, Martha," says Mom. "As long as you don't do it out of being critical, I'd welcome that. And as long as you don't mind me doing the same with you."

"Fine," I say. "I don't mind."

"Fine," says Mom.

4. I tell everyone that my friend Kevin is coming to visit next weekend.

5. We talk about the Stomps murder for a while. Sarah says she heard that someone heard that Hazelynn put her husband through a wood chipper.

"That sounds like that one movie," Dad says.

"*Fargo*," I say. "But it sounds like a rumor to me."

"Maybe Hazelynn saw that movie too," says Mom.

February 22, 2009

(Rachael is back from Mexico. But is not at the meeting. Sarah has made breakfast for Rachael's homecoming. Rachael is gone at a friend's house.)

1. Sarah sets the potatoes down on the table and says she only has a couple complaints this week. "Mom, I don't want you to feel like I'm attacking you, but could you please not leave your socks and earplugs around the house?

Mom says she will try to remember not to do that.

I ask Mom where she would like us to put her earplugs if we find them. She responds that we should put them in the green, ceramic container on the bookshelf.

"What about your socks?" I ask.

"Put them in the laundry."

2. "Dad, I know I can't stop you from putting leftovers in water glasses with a plastic bag over the top, but could you please put them in the door of the fridge, not on the shelf where they fall over and spill?" asks Sarah.

Dad nods.

3. I ask Simone and Sarah to stop leaving half-eaten avocados in the fridge. Sarah says that she never does that. Simone says she will stop doing that.

4. I say that I will attempt to store my urine for my lab tests in a cooler instead of in the fridge.

Everyone thinks that's a good idea.

March 1, 2009

1. The meeting is canceled because everyone has strep throat.

March 8, 2009

1. The Grover family meeting is sabotaged by daylight savings time.

March 15, 2009

1. Sarah and I share with the family that we do all the housework and that no one else does anything. We tell them that we've been writing it down on the calendar on the fridge—when Sarah and I clean the kitchen or pick up the TV room.

"What's your point?" asks Dad.

2. We argue for the next twenty minutes. Mom uses the "f" word. I cry. Sarah says she is emotionally unhealthy in this environment and needs to feel safe in order to be fully actualized as a human being. Dad says he doesn't want to do any housework.

3. We come up with a schedule:

    Kitchen: Saturday – Mom

    Sunday – Simone

    Monday and Tuesday – Martha

    Wednesday – Simone

    Thursday and Friday – Sarah

    TV Room: Sunday – Dad

4. Dad suggests we stop using the words "always" and "never" in family meetings. We agree.

March 22, 2009
1. The meeting is canceled. I'm house-sitting in Sellwood. Sarah is in Seattle.

March 29, 2009
(I am house-sitting so Dad writes the minutes.)

Well okay, Martha is off house-sitting, so she gave Simone the job of writing the family meeting minutes. Now Simone is gone, who knows where, and so the job has fallen to me.

This reminds me of how I ended up with the job of feeding the dogs. Now the dogs are both gone and I don't have to do that anymore. But I want to remind everyone that IF we do get another dog I will have to feed it.

Anyway, we discussed Rachael and Mike coming home and wondered where we were going to put them. And Frani and I decided that there would be no smoking on the porch anymore. Any smoking would have to be done on the street or in cars. This will give Mike some motivation to buy a car or quit smoking. I hope he does both.

There was more talk of if Mike and Rachy were going to go back on the boat and Sarah gave a report about how much everyone on the boat loves them, but burnout might be rearing its ugly head.

Sarah is going on graveyard shift, so she's concerned about her daytime sleep.

I pointed out that anyone using my computer should put it to sleep when they're done.

Frani said something about the yard, but I can't remember what.

There was more discussion about who did and who didn't and who should have emptied and loaded the dishwasher.

There was more, but you know, just boring stuff. No tears or yelling.

April 12, 2009
(Rachael is on her way home from her boyfriend's home. Sarah bought donuts because Mom and Dad were arguing about what kind of donut is the best.)
1. Mom brings up what the consequences of Rachael's absence should be. She also mentions that Rachael hasn't followed the rule of five nights a week at home. (If her stuff is going to be here.)

Sarah states that the issue is really between the parents and Rachael and that they should bring it up with Rachael on their own.
2. Mom thanks Sarah for the yard work she did last week.

"How much did that bigger yard debris bin cost?" Dad wants to know.

"Two more dollars a month," says Sarah.

Dad smiles. "I guess that's not that much."

"Yeah, Mister OOH-it's-going-to-be-too-expensive!" says Mom.

"Just pile it on, dear," says Dad.

3. Mom continues, "Rachael cleaned the bathroom last week, too. She isn't here to get her calcolades ... "

"Accolades?" I say.

"Yes, accolades," Mom says. "Anyway, Mikey is coming home next week and we need to get on the same page so that everyone is as comfortable as possible."

4. Rachael walks in and grabs half an apple fritter from the table.

5. "Who is the last person to bed every night?" asks Dad.

Rachael raises her hand.

"Your job is to walk around and turn off the lights at the end of the night," says Dad.

I bring up the fact that last night I came home and the back door was unlocked. Simone says that she came home last week and the back door was unlocked, "and the front door was wide open!"

6. Sarah complains that people are not rinsing dishes before they put them in the dishwasher. "Cereal bowls!" Mom says, and looks at Dad. "I know it was you—it was Cocoa Krispies."

Dad says he will try to do better.

"A man can only do so much," says Rachael.

"What?" we all groan.

"Rachael, the tables have turned since you last stayed here," says Dad. "But I do want everyone to know that if we had a dog, I would be the one to feed it."

"What?" says Simone.

"We're not getting a dog. That's a joke. That's an old joke," says Sarah.

"I'm just saying that I do do chores around here. That in addition to taking out the garbage, I would feed the dog if we had one," says Dad.

"Yeah, you barely take out the garbage," says Sarah.

"I take out the garbage," says Dad.

"Yeah, but the recycling is out of control," says Sarah.

"I'll try to do a better job," says Dad.

7. Mom goes over a list of extra chores she wants done: dusting, cleaning out the microwave, mowing the lawn, wiping down the cupboards.

8. Sarah reminds Dad that his chore is to clean the TV room on Sundays. "Thanks for reminding me," says Dad.

I apologize to the family for my constant stack of library books and drawing materials in the TV room.

9. We go over everyone's chores for the week.

10. Dad suggests bringing a TV into the living room.

Mom says that no one wants a TV in the living room.

"Don't you already have a TV in your bedroom anyway?" asks Simone.

"Yes," says Dad.

"So you're the only one that wants a TV in this room," I say.

"This carpet is the only carpet that stays clean," says Mom.

"The reason the TV room carpet gets dirty is because there is never a rug in front of the door!" says Dad.

"You have no idea, Mr. Grover!" Mom points her finger at him. "Don't tell me why the carpet is stained! I followed you out of the house the other day and you dripped coffee all the way out of the house! If we put a TV in here it would be covered with coffee stains in a day."

11. Rachael and Mom leave to go to church.

April 19, 2009

1. Sarah says that Rebekah didn't know that the family meetings were mandatory.

"What?" I say. "That's crazy."

"Yeah, she thought that we just do this for fun."

2. Sarah says that Simone doesn't do a very good job of cleaning the kitchen on Wednesdays.

"I did clean the kitchen on Wednesday," says Simone.

"Yeah, but did you wipe off the counters? There was stuff all over the counters and empty wine bottles."

"I don't drink wine," says Simone.

"You can't put an empty bottle in the recycling?"

"I'm sorry. I'll do a better job next time," says Simone.

"Let's just go over what it means to clean the kitchen," I say. "You unload and load the dishwasher and wipe off the counters. You sweep the floors and you wipe down the fronts of the cupboards. You don't have to detail them but if we all do that they will be really clean over time."

"I just get bitter when I go out and spend $50 on groceries and you all eat the food and then don't clean the kitchen on your days," says Sarah.

"I asked you if you wanted money for those groceries," I say. "And you said no."

"I'm not talking about you," says Sarah. "I'm talking about Simone."

"Then don't buy groceries anymore," I say.

"I want to eat what I want to eat," says Sarah. "I want food in the house!"

"Yeah, but that's like saying 'Go ahead and walk all over me because I don't have good boundaries!'" I say.

Dad raises his hand. "Can I just say that Simone, I think you do a great job of cleaning the kitchen."

"Dad, what day does Simone clean the kitchen?" asks Sarah.

"I don't know, but I saw her cleaning it one day and it looked good to me."

3. "Dad, that reminds me—it's very hard to clean the kitchen when there is recycling all over the floor," I say.

"I know. I'll try to do a better job," says Dad.

"There are overflowing glass containers over there," I say.

"I don't recycle beer bottles—stuff that gets a deposit," says Dad.

"We didn't realize that was your system," says Sarah.

"I took all the beer bottles to the store the other day and got $5," says Mom. "And I spent that $5!"

"There is an empty curb container out there today. Did you take it out recently?" says Sarah.

"If you want the neighbors to think you're a good person, you should go to church!" says Mom.

"What? I don't care what the neighbors think. That has nothing to do with it," says Dad.

"Well, the recycling needs to be done," says Sarah.

"Okay. Sorry. I'm a failure," says Dad.

4. Dad brings up a TV in the living room. "I brought this up last week and everyone said 'no,' but Mikey is coming home on Wednesday and we need to do something about the room situation. I don't want people walking through that room when Mike is using it as a bedroom."

Sarah points at Mom and Dad. "This is an issue between you two."

"Dad, it's your and Mom's house and it's your guys' living room," I say. "So do whatever you want. You've already heard all of our reasons why we don't think it's a good idea," I say.

"We've decided it's going to be a flat screen TV," says Mom. "And it's going to be on that wall." She points to the wall next to the fireplace. "That way you can see it from the living room and the kitchen."

"I think you should wait at least two weeks after Mikey gets home before you make a decision," says Sarah.

"It doesn't matter because we don't have the money anyway," says Dad.

5. "Mom, do you have anything to add?" I ask.

"I just would appreciate any help with the yard work," she says. "I got a lot of it done this morning already."

"It's beautiful out there," says Rachael.

"You should spend time out there Dad, it's great," says Sarah.

"I don't go outside," says Dad.

6. Mom is scraping the dead skin off her feet with a special tool. Sarah and Rachael tell her it's disgusting and could she please not do it in the living room.

Mom replies that it's her living room and that fact was already stated earlier in the meeting.

7. Rachael wants her boyfriend to come over for dinner on Tuesday.

8. "Dad, right after the meeting I'm going to go into the TV room and pick up all my stuff so you won't have to when you do your chore today," I say.

"Thanks, Martha," says Dad.

April 26, 2009
(Sarah is asleep in her room because she worked graveyard last night. Mike is back from working on the boat.)

1. I have to be drug out of bed.

2. Mikey is in the living room complaining about how cold it is.

"Okay, Mexico boy," says Dad. "It's not that cold."

3. Mom says that in her absence, Sarah has two orders of business. "Number one," says Mom, "I don't remember. But number two, Sarah says that she bought some toothpaste and she doesn't mind if you use it but she doesn't know where it went."

"I used it, because Mike was in the bathroom showering and I had to brush my teeth," says Simone. "I don't know where it is, but I'll find it."

4. Dad brings up his first order of business. "I want to apologize for not cleaning the TV room. I will try to do a better job of that."

"Can I add something?" Simone raises her hand. "I just want everyone to know that Dad was abducted by aliens on Sunday and that's why he didn't clean the TV room."

"What?" I say.

"Simone, you were only supposed to come up with an excuse if everyone started attacking me," says Dad.

"Oh."

5. Mom brings up the lawn. "I think we're going to buy a riding lawnmower so that the lawn will be easier to mow."

None of us think that a riding lawnmower will solve the problem. We talk about the outside chores for a long time. It's decided that Simone, myself, and Dad don't care about the outside chores. Mom, Mikey, and Sarah will be in charge of the lawn.

"I never go outside," says Dad. "I go outside to get in my truck and drive away. That's when I go outside."

"That's why you don't have any say on how I spend the money!" says Mom. "If you don't care or ever take responsibility for anything having to do with the lawn, then why do you feel like you can sabotage what I'm doing?"

We tell the parents that this is an issue between the two of them.

"What do you think, Rachael?" asks Dad.

Rachael looks up from where she is sleeping on the ground. "What do you mean?"

"I'm just making sure you're still awake."

"Oh yeah," says Rachael and puts her head back down.

6. I tell everyone to try to be quiet at night while I am sleeping. We talk about this for a while. Dad gives me some money to buy a box fan for my room.

7. Dad says that we all need to do better at turning off the lights at night.

8. Mikey says that he doesn't mind if people walk through his room to get to the TV room while he is sleeping. "I won't wake up," he says.

Mom says that she doesn't want to walk in on him while he is getting dressed.

"Then why don't we buy one of those little latches for the door?" asks Mikey.

We all think that is a good idea.

May 3, 2009

1. Mom is folding up the blankets on the living room floor from Ana's kids spending the night last night. Mike complains that she is throwing dust in the air and into his food.

"Mike, there is dust everywhere," I say. "You only see it because she's in front of the window."

Mike storms out of the room. Mom yells after him something about paying rent or it being her house.

We have to coax Mike back into the living room.

"I'm just sensitive to the fact that Mom is cleaning up after the kids, doing the right thing, and you have to criticize her," I say.

"That's what I was thinking!" says Mom.

2. "Okay," says Dad. "I want to start the meeting by stating some minor things. I came home the other day and the door to the garage was wide open."

"The main door?" asks Mike.

"Yes. No biggie. Just minor things. And I think we are all doing a good job of turning off the lights at night."

3. I pull a little latch out of my sweatshirt pocket. "I found this in my room last night," I say. "And I thought it might be good for Mikey to put this on his door when he is changing his clothes so we don't walk in on him. But you have to screw it into the wall and I don't know if you want to do it."

"No," says Dad. "I'll get something else."

I hold up the latch. "Do you want it?"

"No. Throw it away."

"I'm not going to throw it away!" I say. I put it back in my pocket.

4. Mom brings up the beer bottles left over from Mikey's homecoming dinner. Mom doesn't want them sitting on the kitchen floor. She doesn't want them in the curb recycling. Rachael, Mike, and us kids don't think it's worth it to take them back for the refund. Dad points out that we are not a rich family and it's

wasted money not to get the refund. Rachael says it's not worth her time to take them all the way to the grocery store for a handful of change. Mom thinks she could do a lot with that money. "Well," says Rachael, "if you feel so bad, take them back to the grocery store and give them to some homeless person. There's always some skeezy person standing around to give them to."

5. Mom says she needs some help with organization in the house and that one half of the house is completely out of control.

Sarah gets up from where she has been laying on the couch. "I have tried to organize this house so many fucking times and this is what you do to my organization!" Sarah kicks the pile of folded blankets off the coffee table and on to the floor. She kicks the blankets on the floor around. "Every fucking effort to organize! This is what you do to it!"

Dad says he's sorry that Sarah feels that way. "What specifically could we do to be organized?"

"You want some examples?" Sarah lies back down. "Well, you could make the effort to stack the Tupperware before you shove it back in the cupboard. You could fold the blankets before shoving them back in the closet so they don't fall out when you open the door. You could keep me from spending eight hours in your garage moving Martha's stuff so Steve could work on my car."

"What? When were you in my garage?" says Dad.

"Dad, I had to move all that stuff in there, not because I wanted to, but because Steve refused to work on my car unless he could do it in the garage."

"What? When did that happen?" asks Dad.

"Whatever," says Sarah.

"None of this will ever change," says Mikey.

6. I ask Dad if he is going to do his chore of cleaning the TV room.

"Yes, I am going to do that today."

"That's what you said last week and you didn't do it. How can I believe you?"

"I'm getting better and better," says Dad.

"Better and better?" asks Sarah. "You haven't ever done it. How can you get any better?"

"You have no credibility, Mike," says Mom.

Dad says he will pick up the stuff on the floor and vacuum but he won't wipe off the table or clean off his desk. "I have enough on my plate right now," he says. "Let me just conquer this and then I'll add that stuff on to it later."

7. Dad thanks Mikey for mowing the lawn. Mikey points out that the yard debris bin isn't big enough.

8. I ask Mom what explicitly she wants us to do to help her organize the house. She says she wants Mikey to move the boxes out of his room and into the garage. And she wants to get rid of the couch in the TV room.

I don't like that idea.

"That couch is Martha's whole universe," says Mikey.

"Would you really mind that much if we got rid of that couch?" asks Dad.

"Yes, but it's your house and it's your couch so do whatever you want," I say.

9. We talk about the bed situation for ten minutes. Sarah says she will go to Ikea today and buy a bunk bed set if everyone pitches in some money. Dad says he could bring the couch to the dump in Sandy. Rachael and Simone talk about sharing a bed. Simone tells Rachael that Rachael stinks. Rachael tells Simone that Simone is always sweaty.

10. Dad asks Simone if there is anything in the way of her graduating. "Do you have any book fines?" asks Dad.

"No. Corbett doesn't fine you for books," says Simone.

"I still have a book from the fourth grade," says Rachael.

"What was it called?" Mom wants to know.

"*Witches, Witches, Witches.*"

11. Sarah tells Rachael she needs to pick a day that she will clean the bathroom. Rachael picks Wednesday.

12. I say that whoever takes responsibility for babysitting Ana's kids needs to take responsibility for cleaning up after them.

13. Sarah gets up and folds the blankets and stacks them back on the coffee table.

May 10, 2009

1. Dad says he would like it noted in the family meeting minutes that he did clean the TV room last week.

2. Sarah wants to know where we should start putting all the garage sale stuff. "We should have a staging area somewhere for all that stuff," she says. "There are piles of it all over the house."

3. Sarah brings up the fact that Rachael didn't clean the bathrooms this week. "And Mikey," she says. "Is your chore the lawn?"

"Yes," says Mike.

"Well, are you going to do it every week? Because you didn't do it this week."

"Well, it kind of depends on the weather."

"Look," I say. "The point is that we all need to do our chores. Mike needs to mow the lawn, Rachael needs to clean the bathrooms, Mom needs to clean the kitchen."

"I worked all day yesterday," Mom says.

"We could all come up with reasons why we didn't do our chore. I could say, 'Oh, I felt like shit,'" I say.

"We already said that if Mom is busy she needs to ask for help," says Sarah.

"Look, I don't think you guys know how hard we work," says Dad.

"Yes we do," Sarah and I say.

"You've been telling us that for years," says Mike.

"Well I don't need for you to tell us," says Sarah. "I just observe."

4. Dad says something about being irrational and apologizing to Simone.

5. I ask that my laundry be put on my bed if I leave it in the dryer. "I lost two of my towels that I bought because Mom, you put them on the couch and now they're gone forever."

"Well," says Rachael. "The problem is that you take the laundry out of the dryer and you don't always know whose it is."

"There's a lot of magnets on the fridge," says Sarah. "We'll have to start the system where we put our name on the dryer with a magnet."

"Yeah, but the problem with that system is that then people don't take the magnet off and another load gets put in the dryer … and then it just gets all confused," says Dad.

We decide that people will just have to keep track of their own laundry.

"Besides," says Dad, "we have plenty of towels, why didn't you just use our towels?"

"Because," I say, "I want control. And it worked fine for nine months."

6. I ask that people not take the magazines I have placed on the bathroom counter out of the bathroom. "But what if they're interesting?" Mom wants to know.

7. The meeting is adjourned because Sarah and Rachael have to go to work.

May 17, 2009

(Mikey and Rachael are gone camping.)

1. Mom, Sarah, and Simone are making a guest list for Simone and Sarah's graduation party.

2. Sarah is upset that Rachael has only cleaned the bathroom once since she moved back in.

"Yeah, that bathroom is disgusting," I say.

"I'm just upset because I have been paying a bill and doing my chores and they aren't doing anything," says Sarah.

"I just have a problem that Mikey sleeps all day," says Mom.

"Well, it wouldn't be a problem if he actually did his chores," I say.

"Yeah. Who cares if he sleeps all day—just do your freakin' chore," says Sarah.

"I don't know why, but it really bothers me," says Mom.

"Rachael sleeps all day too," says Sarah.

"Yeah, but Rachael is behind a closed door!" says Mom.

Dad and Simone don't say anything.

"Mike," says Mom. "We need your leadership here. We need you to put aside your feelings of guilt about their irresponsibility. That's counter-productive. Just pretend they aren't your kids. Can you do that? It's not your fault that they are taking advantage. This all rests on your shoulders now to say something to them."

"It's not all on your shoulders," I say. "But we do need your help."

"Okay," says Dad.

"I was gonna say that we should help Dad clean the TV room today, but all that stuff is Rachael's. And now she's not here," I say.

3. Mom brings out her calendar and goes over her plans for the week. She also says that she needs help with some open houses in Bridal Veil because Dad will be working graveyard this summer. I volunteer for one weekend in July. Sarah says she will try to do one weekend but she can't be sure because of her work schedule.

"How about you, Simone?" asks Mom.

"What? I wasn't listening," says Simone.

4. "Does anyone have anything else?" I say.

5. "I just have a minor thing," says Dad. "My computer has power supply issues and sometimes that power strip gets pulled away from the wall and gets under the computer chair. So just be careful with that."

"That's my fault," I say. "I plug in my laptop a lot. I'll try not to do that anymore."

6. I bring up people not taking my zines out of the bathroom. "Did I already ask that at the last meeting?" I say.

"Yeah you did," says Sarah.

7. "So Dad, what are you going to say to Rachael and Mikey when they get home?" I ask.

"I'm going to say, Rachael—you need to clean the bathroom, Mike—you need to mow the lawn, and both of you need to check in before you miss a family meeting."

I give Dad the thumbs up.

8. "Is this meeting over?" asks Simone. "I need to go back to bed."

May 24, 2009

Martha begins by asking who will write the minutes.

Dad says, "Are you saying you don't want to do the minutes because you've got nothing more to say?"

"I just need a break," Martha says. Mom says she'll write them. Martha asks me (Sarah) to since I never have. "That way, everyone will take a turn."

Mike is camping with Zoe and Simone is at Sasquatch.

1. At 9:30 Rachael is in the kitchen making her breakfast. I complain that all members should be in the living room for the meeting—that shouting from the kitchen doesn't count as being at the meeting. Rachael counters with, "Before you were here, the meetings were just joking around for an hour."

I say, "Didn't you tell me you used to cry at every meeting?"

The discussion continues with Dad making the point that it doesn't need to be so militant. Martha says she sometimes has a hard time getting out of bed in the morning. I tell her she can always use the Martha clause. The family eventually agrees that I am getting too upset and making it too big of a deal. I point out that I am not upset and angry—that my voice just sounds that way.

"Mine always does, too," Dad says.

2. I go over a few things Mikey wanted me to talk about at the meeting. Dad's pile of stuff under the tree in the yard, Mom's plant-buying compulsion, everyone keeping the yard mess to a minimum until after me and Simone's graduation party. "Dad, Mike wants me to talk to you about your pile of crap behind you."

Dad turns around on the ottoman to see the plastic container on the hearth. It's overflowing with CD spindles and other electronic equipment. "He says you said you were going to get rid of that and all your other stuff in his closet so he can clean his room. Can he just throw it away?"

"Do you really want to throw away the Atari?" Dad says.

There is a moment of silence and everyone looks at me. "I guess."

3. Martha talks about her trip to California, how Rachael is going to help her move down there.

4. Mom asks Rachael what her plans are this summer. Rach says, "Well ... Simone's graduation, the party, then I am going to help Martha move."

5. I tell Martha that Judy loved her story about Thanksgiving and that she thought it should be on *This American Life*. This starts Dad and Martha on a bitter tirade about how the show is just nepotism and all about Chicago, etc. Dad says, "Sometimes you turn it on and it's not even real. It's some story someone wrote."

This leads into a general discussion of under what circumstances it's okay to listen to fiction.

6. Mom talks about her book club that is coming to the house this week. She needs help with the boxes of dishes on the dining room floor. She also asks Dad to deal with the recycling.

7. I complain about the parking. Simone is a close parker. We talk for fifteen minutes about the best parking configuration if Mikey buys a car, which would bring us to eight cars in the driveway. Someone would have to be blocked in. Dad is the most adamant with his ideas so eventually we all agree with him.

8. Mom's book club is reading *Wild Swans,* a book about China. The conversation dissolves into a discussion about Mao and Rachael leaves the room. Dad decides we should all do some stretches. He leads the three of us in a routine he does at the job site every morning. We decide that we are going to start the meetings with this routine from here on out.

May 31, 2009
I am still sick of writing the minutes. This is the meeting in Mikey's words.

At 9:29 Sarah sits in the living room singing "Beauty and the Beast." Mom makes up the "sock song" while dumping additional laundry on top of a pre-existing pile on the love seat. Starts folding. Everyone convenes at the usual time.

1. Mom starts by suggesting we go around saying what we're thankful for—pointing out that all we ever talk about are our grievances. She says that she is thankful for the house and that she is able to provide for all of us.

Martha: Everyone that's in the room. You've all helped me a lot over the past months.

Sarah: I'm thankful for my hiking partner (she asks me to leave out some comments she thinks sound suggestive) Heidi.

Me: (After half a minute of stuttering) Life, living, all of it.

Dad: Oh! Can I piggyback on that answer? Mike just about summed it up.

Rachael: (Squeaking out of her impromptu fleece cocoon on the floor) Surprisingly ... living here.

Simone: Thirteen years of free education.

2. Sarah starts off grievances by mentioning Simone's habit of parking too close to everyone else.

Rachael, "Yeah, you park weird."

Martha, "You're a close parker."

Back to Sarah with, "You should practice parking."

"Maybe she just does it because she can," I suggest. Simone finds this entertaining, no on else does.

3. Mom asks Simone if she's going to Maggie's graduation party in the afternoon. Simone has to work and can't make it.

"Well, you and I should go." She looks at Dad. "I'd like to give her some money." Simone interjects, "No, don't give her money! They're not giving me anything."

"I'm not going to go to that," Dad says. "It's at Maggie's house? No. No, I'm not going; there won't be any parking."

It's decided that no one will go.

4. Mom says she's going to try not to look at us as her kids and that we try in return not to look at her as a parent.

5. Sarah doesn't want us to make plans the week before her party so that we can help around the house and yard.

"I'm not going to clean the living room a week before the party," she explains. "I have to do it right before the party. I know how you all are."

I then make the mistake of saying that we wouldn't be the way we are if we would clean our dishes as we dirty them. After being on the boat for six months I have forgotten the implications of this statement.

(I have made this statement to no avail in the past.)

"I know we have a system worked out so that someone cleans them everyday, but it's not that hard to clean them as you use them," I say.

Dad interrupts me. "I know you think that you're making sense but let me just correct you here. We don't live in your fantasy-land, you'd be better off saying that you're going to walk around the house picking up after everyone else. In short, just do it. Like the Nike slogan."

I then make a tactical backtrack and say, "All I was trying to say is it would be more respectful to the person who cleaned the kitchen any given day if we tried to maintain some of that."

Everyone seems appeased by this.

6. Mom says we should start getting our rooms clean and try to keep them that way. Sarah asks, "Have you guys ever had sheets on your bed? I tried to recall but I can't remember either way."

"Well, what happens is we take them off to clean them and go about our days," says Dad.

"By the time we get back to them it's late," says Mom.

"We're tired, and, you know—" says Dad.

Martha then interjects, "So, in other words, no—you don't use sheets."

June 7, 2009
No Meeting!

June 14, 2009
(It's 10:30 a.m. Last night was Sarah and Simone's graduation party. Dad, Sarah, Simone, Mom, Maggie and myself are sitting in the living room talking about the party. Rachael walks in. "Are we having the meeting?" she asks. Maggie gets up and walks out of the room. "I'm going back to bed," she says. "Maggie! You can stay," says Mom. Maggie keeps walking.)

June 21, 2009
(Dad is at work this morning)

1. "I'm gonna pull a Rachael today and sleep through the meeting," says Mikey, and lays down on the ground.

2. "Your father gave me an assignment in his absence." Mom pulls out the electrical bill. "Last month the electric bill was $98. This month the electric bill was $150. We all need to do a better job of turning off the lights."

"I came home the other night and every single light in the house was on," says Sarah.

"I went to take a nap the other day and all the lights were off," says Mom. "And then I got up and all the lights were on again." We all agree to do a better job of turning the lights off at night.

3. Mom says to me that the kitchen table cannot turn into a place for me to put my stuff. "Your plants were on the table for four days," she says. "And you left all that food there last night."

I agree to not leave my stuff on the table.

4. I ask everyone when they're going to help me get stuff ready for the garage sale. Sarah says she is helping Grandma all day on Tuesday with Mike and Rachael. I also want to know what all the crap in the garage is.

"I went down there the other day," I say. "And there was just all this stuff everywhere and I don't know what's what."

5. Sarah asks us if we know the fundamentals of microbiology and why we shouldn't be using each other's razors.

"I have a razor with four blades," says Rachael.

"I keep my razor under the sink," says Mikey.

"My razor vibrates," says Simone.

"I keep my BLUE razor on the right hand side of the shower," says Sarah.

"Well, I've been using that razor," I say.

"Did you buy that razor?" asks Sarah.

"Well, no. But I've bought a lot of razors at some point, although I don't know what color they are, or where they are."

"Well, stop using that one," says Sarah.

"Okay, but I just want to let you know that I replace it with a fresh one often and I wasn't doing it on purpose."

"Okay," says Sarah.

6. Sarah wants to know what the parking situation is. "Now that we have five cars for the upper lot, how do we want to do this?"

No one says anything.

"Have we decided that whoever is the last one in just parks on the street?"

7. Rachael asks if she can go back to bed.

8. Mom starts to tell us about her dream.

"Is this meeting over?" asks Sarah.

9. Sarah and Rachael and Mikey leave the room.

Simone, Mom, and I tell each other about our dreams.

July 5, 2009

(Zoe spent the night. Rachael is MIA.)

1. Simone cuts her eggs and takes a bite. "I should have said this earlier but I have to leave soon. Could we start the meeting?"

"Where are you going?" I ask.

"I'm going to Sunriver," she says.

"Who's doing your chores while you're gone?" asks Sarah.

"What are your days?" I ask.

"Wednesday and yesterday," says Simone.

"I'll do Wednesday," I say.

"Why doesn't Mike take Wednesday since he hasn't mowed the lawn in weeks?" Sarah wants to know.

Dad looks at Mike. "Will you mow the lawn today?"

Mike rubs his hands over his face. "No."

"Why not?"

"Because. Look at my hand." Mike opens up his left hand.

"What happened to your hand?" asks Dad.

"I was wrestling Dan last night and I grabbed what I thought was a branch but it was a blackberry bush. Instead of letting go, though, he pulled me forward and I held on and the thing scratched my hand really bad," says Mike, making a sweeping motion with his hand.

"You must have been pretty numb," says Mom.

"Drunk," says Mike. "Why can't you just say what you mean?" He looks at Dad. "I have to work today."

"Will you mow the lawn tomorrow?" asks Dad.

Mike nods.

"Are you still cool with doing the kitchen on Wednesday?" I ask.

Mike nods.

2. "I'm really annoyed that Rachael isn't here," says Sarah. "She's supposed to clean the bathrooms. I almost feel like it would be easier to keep her doing her chores if she did the kitchen one day."

"She picked a day for her chore," says Simone. "She's supposed to clean the bathrooms on Wednesday."

3. "Hasan wanted everyone to know that he wants the Grover drink to be Black Velvet," I say. "He said that was his two cents for the meeting."

"Does he know that's what my dad used to drink all the time?" asks Dad. "Why would he say that?"

"I'm sure he didn't mean anything by it," says Mom.

4. Dad says that he came home the other day and the air conditioning was on and the front door was open. "Wide open," he says.

We all agree to make sure the house is shut if the air conditioning is on.

5. I ask for help moving some boxes in my room so I can vacuum.

6. "I also think it's funny that we got rid of all that stuff at the garage sale and then you guys got all this crap!" I point at the new lamp in the living room and the new couch on the lawn.

Mom throws up her hands, "We didn't even get rid of that much stuff! There's still a bunch of stuff down in the garage!"

Dad looks at me. "Yeah, I know."

July 12, 2009

1. "I just want to apologize for all this art crap here," I say, pointing at the boxes of art supplies on the coffee table and the floor of the living room.

2. Mom and Dad start talking about Mom's new computer that just froze up.

Dad suggests she buy a new computer instead of buying a used or refurbished one again.

"I would gladly go buy a new one in a second," says Mom. "But it's gonna cost me!"

"I realize this is important," says Sarah. "But do we need to talk about this at the meeting?"

"It's gonna cost at least $200 more than a used computer," Mom goes on.

"Mom, you sound sick," says Rachael.

"I know. And I got it from him!" Mom points at Dad.

3. Mikey points out that before anyone accuses him of having no chores or doing anything around the house that they realize that he will do what people ask if they ask him to do it "right now."

"Like, if you ask me—will you help some lady move and get two friends of yours to help—on such and such a day—then you have to remind me the day of. Not a couple days before. I forget."

I point out that Mike says this but often times when I do ask him to do something right now he says, "No."

"Well maybe I'm in the middle of something," says Mike.

"Well, I don't understand what you're saying. It doesn't make any sense," I say.

"I don't know why you're getting so defensive Martha. I'm just telling you how I am. If anyone is an expert on ME, it's me. Right?"

Mom raises her hand, "I know something that none of the rest of you know. So you have to listen to me!"

"What?"

"Have any of you read *Men are from Mars, Women are from Venus?*"

"You've brought that up before," I say. "Look. I'm just trying to treat you how I want to be treated. If you ask me to do something the day of—well I've already made plans by that time."

"I'm not that way," says Mike. "Don't ask me ahead of time. If you ask me that day—I'll do it."

"Will you clean the bathrooms?" asks Rachael.

"When?" asks Mike.

"Today."

"I'll clean that one," says Mike pointing to the hallway.

"Hey! Why are you letting her steamroll you into doing her chore?" Simone wants to know.

"Because he has to maintain his position!" says Rachael.

Rachael and I laugh.

4. "It was my day to clean the kitchen yesterday," says Mom. "And I didn't do it."

"Wait, I thought you and Simone switched," says Sarah.

"We switched, and then you and I switched," says Simone.

"Whose day is it today?" asks Sarah.

"It's Simone's day," says Mom.

"Don't try and shove the kitchen on your Mom," says Dad. "She has a lot of stuff on her plate."

"Mike! Stay out of it!" says Mom.

It's decided that Simone and Sarah will clean the kitchen.

5. I ask Rachael if she wants to take a scenic route down to San Francisco.

"Sure," she says.

Dad expresses concern that we won't be able to move me into my new apartment without help.

Sarah says that Rachael is pretty strong and that as women we are used to asking for help.

I assure Dad that we will be fine.

6. Mom wants to know if anyone can accompany her to Salem to get her computer fixed. We are all busy.

7. "Why are there so many phones on that chair?" Dad wants to know. Mom gets up and starts disconnecting one of the old phones from its wires.

"Look, I know that phone was only a dollar, but do we really need that many phones?" asks Dad.

"I don't answer that phone because there isn't any caller ID," says Sarah.

"None of you ever answer the phone!" says Mom. "You never, never answer the phone! I was trying to reach your dad yesterday. He didn't answer his cell and I had JUST left the house. There were FIVE people here and none of you answered the phone!!"

"I was sleeping," says Dad.

"I never answer the phone unless it's you or Dad," says Simone.

"Or Grandma," says Sarah.

"Yeah, or Grandma," says Simone.

"What are these wires?" Mom asks pointing at two wires coming out of the back of the phone.

"Those are like those things that lobsters have," says Dad.

July 19, 2009

1. Mom brings in a Tupperware container of blueberries.

"Where did those come from?" asks Sarah.

"From our garden," says Dad.

"Garden?" I say.

2. Mom starts off the meeting by showing us three empty beer bottles and a used match. "I thought there was nothing worse than cigarette butts in the yard. But I actually hate this worse: beer bottles all over the property. And they're full of cigarettes butts!"

Mom holds them up.

3. Dad points at Mike. "You're getting back on the boat in October." He points at Rachael. "You're moving down to Eugene in September." He points at me. "You're moving out on the 29th?"

We nod.

"I know you guys aren't going to like this, but if any of you move back in, you will move back in as non-smokers. Not just no smoking at home. But you CANNOT be a smoker and live here."

"Okay," I say.

"That's perfectly reasonable," says Mike.

4. I ask Mom if she has anything else to add.

"There are flowers growing in the lawn," she says. "That means that the lawn hasn't been mowed for a loooong time."

5. "Yeah," says Sarah. "These three haven't been doing their chores." She points at Mike, Dad, and Rachael.

Dad looks at Mike. "Are you going to mow the lawn today?"

"Yeah, after a nap," Mike says.

"I didn't do my chore last week," says Rachael. "Or the week before."

"I've only done my chore once," says Dad.

"Yeah, I haven't wanted to nag you about it since you work every weekend and are so tired," I say.

"I'll help you do it, Dad," says Sarah.

6. I tell everyone that I will be having friends over for a dinner on Friday. I also remind them that I'll be compiling all the meeting minutes to put them together for a zine. "And I want all your input," I say. "200 words. It could be reflective about what this year has meant for you, or it could be something stupid and irrelevant—whatever you want."

"Only Mikey's will be stupid and irrelevant," says Simone.

"Simone, it's good to hear you chime in!" says Mom.

"That was a left-handed compliment if I ever heard one," says Dad.

"Well, isn't that what family meetings are all about? Making jabs at each other?" asks Mom.

"Yeah, fuck you all!!" says Mike, and laughs.

7. Sarah gets up and walks away.

8. "Is the meeting over?" asks Mike. "I'm going back to bed."

"Good," I say. "You're grouchy."

"No, you guys are all grouchy," says Mike.

July 27, 2009

(Zoe spent the night.)

1. Dad starts off the meeting by telling Zoe what "beautiful white legs" she has.

"We all have pretty white legs," says Sarah.

"Let's see the boy's legs!" says Mom.

Mikey is asleep on the floor and doesn't respond.

2. Zoe tells me that the Steenson girls read the family meeting minutes online.

"No one is going to read my blog after I move," I say.

"Yeah, who is going to do the minutes after you leave?" asks Mom.

"No one does them as well as you," says Rachael. "You always remember everything."

"I always forget what we talk about at the meeting," says Dad.

"I think that's pretty obvious," I say.

3. Sarah asks who left all the dirty laundry all over the bathroom floor.

"Oh, I guess that was me," Mom says.

4. Sarah also wants to know who will do my chores after I move to San Francisco.

It's decided that Rachael will do the kitchen after I move out.

"And then I won't have to do the bathrooms," she says.

"You don't do them anyway!" says Sarah.

"I did them a couple times. And then I forgot—until you reminded me."

5. Mom gets up and starts to go through the drawer in the buffet. She pulls out an outdoor thermometer. "Look at where this was!" she says.

"Is the meeting over?" I ask. "I want all of your opinions on the minutes over the last year. What you think about it, etc. Just e-mail me. 200 words."

Sarah says that she needs a deadline.

"Okay, the deadline is the end of August."

6. Mom has pulled the contents of the buffet drawer out onto the table and has left the room.

"Is the meeting over?" I ask. "Where did Mom go?"

Dad looks down at the coffee table. "I know I had something I was really upset about that I wanted to bring up, but now I can't remember. Oh well, I guess it wasn't that important."

Here are their reflections:

DAD: Having a weekly family meeting is really one of the best ideas I've ever had, even if Frani said it was really her idea. It's a good way to communicate all those little things you want to tell people, but always forget. It also lets everyone get things off their chests before they become big things.

I was a little embarrassed to see certain things appear on Martha's blog. But what could I say? They were true. I think the one thing you wouldn't know by reading the minutes is that someone cried almost every week, and there was some fierce resentment towards anyone that didn't show up for the meeting.

It was a great time, and I already miss the little birds that are flying the nest.

MOM: Martha has forced me to acknowledge that my family does not necessarily believe everything I have attempted to teach them. She's made me face that my edition of the way things are is not the only edition. Verbal communication can be easily edited, forgotten, and discounted. The written word is a very different animal. It's permanent, finite, and infinite, all at the same time. Although her family meeting minutes have not always communicated the way I perceived our meetings, I have mostly been unable to argue with her interpretation. And I'm usually just grateful for her mercy, I mean in light of the reality that she's going to write them and publish them anyway.

ANA: I never thought I would be one of those parents who "couldn't wait for school to start again." I mean, why have kids if you can't wait to get rid of them? Last year changed all that for me. My oldest, Amelia, entered 2nd grade, and Charlie, my second, entered kindergarten. This left just the four-year-old Ada and me at home, four days a week, eight hours a day. Suddenly, my laundry was folded and put away, and there were warm cookies on the table for an after school snack.

I went on the field trips, Ada and I became fixtures in Charlie's class, and we had lunch with Amelia. My children were gaining knowledge and independence through the classic American rite of passage: elementary school. First I had bore them and then weaned them, they had spent their first nights away and they were gaining self-confidence. All of these steps were leading to the day when I would watch them pack up and move out, start their own lives, go to college, get married, and at least generally no longer be my responsibility.

Then sometime after Halloween last year Martha mentioned the Grover Family Meeting Minutes. I went online and read them and my world came crashing down.

"'So, Martha and I were right—that it would get damaged outside,' Sarah says with a smile.

'With some hesitation, Dad admits that yes, we were right.'" (From the November 2nd minutes.)

I was hooked. I was mortified. My parents, who had only one minor child left, still had five children living with them, all of them with the needs and desires of adults. But what really surprised me is how the minutes showed how the children were still just that: children! They were insistent, thoughtless, bossy, critical, entitled, and needy. My parents were still responsible for them! And as much as I would like to deny the possibility, there was a chance that this too could happen to me! In fact, the writing was on the wall: your children are ALWAYS your children! Not that I wanted to get rid of them, I had just hoped for a time when I could stop explaining "why" I live my life a certain way, and "why" I think they should do the same. I thought there would be a time far off down the road, when Chad and I would be just the two of us, heading out on life's next adventure.

These minutes and all the information in them has changed the way I look at my family. I have felt like an outsider. Coming from a large family it's hard to know what's happening in the day-to-day of your siblings' and parents' lives. However, when seven out of nine are living together, they have a bit of an advantage of staying in touch, so in some ways, I've been jealous. However, I have definitely not envied the adult children their seemingly pointless attempts to change the habits of their parents, or their own personal struggles that have kept them living there in the first place.

For all the laughs, the cups of coffee, the interesting conversations, and the late night glasses of wine, I wish I had been there with all of you: Mom, Dad, Sarah, Martha, Rachael, Mike, and Simone. But, according to the minutes, I'm glad I missed the meetings!

SARAH: Living with Martha as an adult was a treat. By the time she got here I'd been swimming against the current of my family for a year. Many of her early issues at meetings were my issues. And by that time the family had weakened my resolve. I think Martha was better at getting results—maybe because she is more rational, or that she had the strength of her helplessness to influence the others. Reading the minutes to the meetings always made me feel better about the meetings. Martha is good at pointing out the ridiculous humor in our exchanges. Also, I felt like she was pretty fair, gentle even, with us. She never made me sound as crazy as I sound to myself—a point that I've shared with friends who commonly respond, "Really?"

ZOE: My family enjoys making a spectacle of themselves. The Grover Family Meeting Minutes are just one more example of this.

RACHAEL, MIKE, AND SIMONE:

Rachael: Hey Mike—what are you going to write about for that thing Martha wants?

Mike: I don't know. I've been putting it off forever. I probably won't even do it.

Rachael: You should do it. Jeez, it'll just take a minute of your precious time.

Mike: Have you done anything yet?

Rachael: Nope. Don't plan on it.

Mike: Do you just want me to do it so you don't have to?

Rachael: No, I was kidding. I'm going to do it. I already know everything I'm going to write, too.

Mike: If I knew what I was going to write, I'd be done already. But I don't know what to write.

Rachael: I just thought I'd write about the old family meetings.

Mike: Like back before Sarah and Martha moved back in?

Rachael: Yeah, the good old days of family meetings.

Mike: It was great because back then anything serious that came up would be shot down immediately by a round of non-sequiturs.

Rachael: I don't even remember anything serious coming up.

Mike: Well, if you consider breaking curfew and not mowing the lawn serious, that's what I'm referring to.

Rachael: Oh yeah. Yeah, I remember mostly their concerns of our late arrivals. Though really, looking back, I shouldn't have been so reactionary, they had every right to be concerned. I was out smoking pot and getting drunk until 4:00 a.m., which is also probably why I was so reactionary.

Mike: Yeah. And I flew under the radar a lot more than you did. You started becoming more and more dramatic as the meetings went on and then you moved out.

Rachael: Well, I do remember saying, "Fuck you" to Mom and Dad and then running into my room and slamming the door. But if memory serves, I think I did that because they told me to be home at 2:00 a.m. rather than 5:00 a.m. Or maybe it was that I needed to go back to school. And flying under the radar, my ass! They just didn't care about what you did.

Mike: It's because I was in a relationship. *(He laughs.)*

Rachael: What?!! I was in several! *(She laughs.)*

Mike: I was on Adderall, depressed, and going to driver's ed. I was unhappy and naturally Mom and Dad knew. Why would they pick on me?

Rachael: So was I! What about Simone, what was she doing at those meetings?

Simone: What am I ever doing at those meetings? Sitting obediently, waiting for it to end.

Rachael: Well, the new meetings were liked turned tables. The kids now lecturing the parents about chores.

Simone: Yeah, it was awesome.

Mike: And now everyone is moving out. It will just be Mom, Dad, and Sarah. Do you think they will still have the meetings?

Rachael: Well, probably. I'm sure Sarah will still want to sit them down.

Mike: They'll probably be a lot more calm.

Simone: I guess, but don't you think the only people who ever yell are Mom, Dad, and Sarah?

Rachael: Yeah, you're right. Hey Simone! Good news—tomorrow is our last family meeting!

(Dad comes into the room saying YAHOO!)

Simone: Last family meeting until one of us runs out of money and has to come back.

Dad: Simone, hopefully when you come back we'll have a place for you.

Mike: Yeah, where Dot (the old dog) slept in the entryway.

Simone: Rachael, I'm going to need my work pants.

Rachael: Can we just stay on topic here?

Sarah *(from the kitchen)*: Man, I can just not get to work on time!

Dad: That's because no one is making you get to work on time.

Mike: I always get to work on time.

Dad: By the way, do you think that shorts that have something written across the butt seem a little gauche to you?

Sarah: Gauche?

Dad: Gauche is like no taste.

Sarah: Trashy.

Rachael: Yeah, and the weird thing is it's always young girls. What parents are letting their thirteen-year-old daughter wear pants with bright pink sparkly letters saying "princess" across her ass?

Dad: Good question.

Rachael: Mike! Simone!

Mike: Yeah, what's up?

Rachael: Come back in here. We need to finish.

Dad: I can eat crunchy watermelon that's not that sweet but I cannot eat mushy watermelon that's sweet.

Mike: I know.

Simone: Me too.

Rachael: Well, I guess this is what I'm going to give Martha.

(No one responds. Dad starts in on a story about a man he showed a house to.)

Pee-Hat

I'M USED TO IT by now: all my doodads and thingamabobs, all the
medical jargon and dosage information. I can talk hormones with
any old endocrinologist. I can chat up diabetics endlessly about
glucose and blood sugar dives. I can rattle off different opiates and
milligrams with any pill-popper down the block. But one thing I
haven't ever needed a name for is my pee-hat. It's a white plastic
container that fits over the toilet to catch my pee. I use it for the
marathon urine collections I have to do for the drug study. I call it
a pee-hat because if you turn the thing over, it looks like a hat—the
kind of hat you would never want to wear, but a hat nonetheless.

In my new apartment in San Francisco I unpack my needles and
syringes, my sharps containers, my urine jugs, my medications. But
after setting up my clothes and dresser, buying fancy glass jars for
my needle-heads, and tacking a shower caddy and a red basket to
the wall for all my drugs, I realize I've left the pee-hat in Oregon.

I call my sister to see if she can send it down to me. She's in the
middle of painting my brother's old bedroom.

"Um, Sarah. I was wondering if you could do me a favor?" I say.

"What's up?"

"I forgot to pack my urine collection thingies. Not the jugs, but
the hat thing that fits over the toilet. There were two of them—"

Sarah sighs into the phone. "I know what you're talking about.

I threw one of them away. You left them under the sink in the bathroom. They still had pee all over them. You could have at least rinsed them off!"

I have no excuse for this. "Um yeah. Sorry about that. Could you send the other one down?"

"Martha, it will probably cost just as much for me to send one down as it would for you to buy a new one. Can't you just buy a new one?"

I wonder bitterly why Sarah has to be so logical all the time. I also wonder where the hell I'm going to find a pee-hat. I get on the Internet and start calling medical supply stores.

"Hi," I say. "I'm looking for a container that fits over the toilet that you collect your urine in."

"What?" a lady says.

"It's white. It's like a hat."

"A bed pan?"

"No, it's not a bed pan. It's for when you have to collect a lot of urine. You put it on the toilet and pee into it and then you dump the urine into a jug."

Silence on the other end of the phone. I wonder if the lady thinks that because I keep using the word "you" I'm accusing her of doing such an odd and grotesque activity herself.

"I don't know what you're talking about," she says.

I search the Internet for another store and find one that has helpfully listed all their products on their website. I don't see "pee-hat" anywhere but they do carry colostomy bags and "specimen containers" so I figure it's worth a shot. I call the store and a man answers the phone.

"Hi," I say. "I'm on your website right now and I notice that you have specimen containers listed here and I was wondering if you had a container for collecting your own urine. It fits over the toilet … "

"Is it white?" the man says.

"Yeah."

"Does it look like a hat?"

"Yes!" I say.

"Yeah, we have 'em. $5."

"Great," I say. "I'll come tomorrow." I'm overjoyed. I feel as though I've found my long lost child.

I look up my bus route on Google Maps and head out the next afternoon. I'm supposed to take the 44 and get off at Sixth and Clement. I have it all written down on a scrap of paper. I leave the house without my map, feeling confident that I can at least board the bus headed in the right direction: towards downtown, past Golden Gate park, and north a couple blocks to Sixth and Clement. But when I get down to the bus station I realize that my internal compass is a bit wobbly. I realize I don't really know which direction downtown is. A thirteen-year-old girl stands at the bus station, chewing bubble gum and listening to her iPod.

"Hi," I say. "Does the 44 head downtown here? Or do I need to board on the other side of the street?"

She doesn't take out her earphones, just looks at me the way thirteen-year-old girls look at tubby older women. I think she nods. The 44 arrives two seconds later, so I get on.

After 40 minutes, one other white woman and I are the last ones on the bus. She's looking around. She looks confused, too. "Last stop," the bus driver says.

I walk up with my scrap of paper in my hand. "I think I got on the wrong bus," I say to the driver.

She laughs. "Yeah, I saw you back there, and I thought you'd gotten on the wrong bus. Are you trying to get to the museums?"

I'm baffled by this. I want to say, "No, I'm in search of a pee-hat." Or, "How could you tell?" Or, "What museums?" Or "Is it because I'm white?" Instead I say, "I need to get to Sixth and Clement."

"Sit down and make yourself comfortable," she says. "That's on the other end of my route."

And it really is "her" route. Most of the riders for the next couple stops seem to know her and each other. She even lets one of them, a bony, drunk-looking woman, ride for free.

Back we go. We're in no man's land: out near a port and a golf course, an industrial-looking post office. I should have known I was headed in the wrong direction. But what do I know? Not enough to even rinse my own urine off my own pee-hat, apparently.

I've been on the bus for over an hour now. My blood sugar is starting to dive and luckily I've brought along some trail mix and cookies. But I keep staring at a sign above the driver. No eating, smoking, or radios, it says. The sign shows a soda and a hot dog with an x through them. A hot dog actually looks pretty good right now. I remember I have some Vitamin Water with me. I could just drink it, I think. I wonder how strict they are with the rules.

The bus driver hangs up her cell phone and starts to dig around in a plastic bag. I'm starting to get sweaty and shaky. When she pulls out some orange juice, I figure I'm okay. I time my gulps with hers so that we are both drinking at the same time. At least if she tries to bust me she'll look like a total hypocrite. The whole thing is beginning to irritate me. What if I was diabetic? I might as well be a diabetic, I start grumbling to myself. I wish I'd brought my cane with me because I keep getting the evil eye when I don't give up my seat to old ladies.

We pass my original bus stop and go up a windy hill, past a reservoir and a suburban-looking strip mall. Soon we are driving through Golden Gate Park and I see what the driver was referring to: the Botanical Garden and some other museums. Do I look like a tourist? I definitely look like I don't know what the hell is going on.

We exit the park and drive into a neighborhood filled with Asian markets and trendy coffee shops.

"Sixth and Clement," the driver says.

I see the medical supply store's blue awning. After thanking the driver, I get off the bus. The man at the counter is talking on the phone when I walk in. I look around the crowded store for my pee-hat. Blood sugar monitors, ankle braces, and all varieties of crutches and stethoscopes line the walls. Wheelchairs, canes, and walkers are gathered together in the middle of the room. I don't see a pee-hat anywhere.

The man puts down the phone. "Can I help you find something?"

"I'm looking for a plastic container that fits over your toilet. You collect your pee in it."

"Oh, yes," the man says, not at all horrified by the description. He turns around and digs into a closet behind the register. He pulls out a pee-hat from a pile of strange plastic containers. I'm so glad to see my pee-hat that I don't even notice what the other containers look like. Only later do I wonder what they're all about—what strange uses they may have. Whose lost children they may be.

"This is a very unique product," he says as he rings me up. "Did your doctor tell you about this?"

"No—I left mine back in Oregon."

"Yes, this is a very special product. Usually only doctors order these."

"I know," I say. "I had a hard time finding one. You guys were the only ones who carried it."

The man smiles as he places the pee-hat and my receipt in a bag. "Be sure to tell all your friends!"

We laugh. "Thanks," I say.

Visual Check

FOR THIS VISIT back home I'm traveling with two jugs of my own urine. At 10:30 p.m., at the San Francisco airport, I scoot my duffel bag along the ground with my foot. My arms are occupied with my jacket, my purse, my boarding pass, my ID, and a note from OHSU stating that I am a drug trial patient whose carry-on baggage consists of small unmarked vials of medication and large jugs of urine. The note states that these items are medically necessary and are not bomb-making materials such as Axe body spray, holy water, or toothpaste.

As I approach the gates, the sound of the gray plastic bins being thrown onto the conveyor belt grows more and more percussive. Up ahead, people are bending over to remove their shoes and placing their belongings on the conveyor belt that leads into the x-ray machine. Now it's my turn. The line that was moving too slow just moments ago is now moving too fast. I hurriedly yank off my shoes and throw my purse, jacket, and duffel bag onto the conveyor belt. I hold onto my ID and the note from OHSU. If they give me any shit, I tell myself, I have the note explaining everything.

The man on the other side of the metal detector motions me through. I obey and the alarm goes off. "Do you have anything under that?" he asks, pointing at my black sweatshirt.

"Just my bra," I say, thinking he means anything metal.

MARTHA GROVER

He sighs and motions me into a four-by-four foot area bordered with the zip pull cables that divide up most of the airport. A couple more people set off the alarm and suddenly I'm standing with three other confused travelers inside the rope, all of us clutching something—an ID, a wallet, a jacket.

"Whose bag is this?" A young security officer is holding up my teal duffel bag.

"It's urine for a drug trial," I say. "I have a note." I hold up the folded piece of computer paper.

"Follow me," the young man says. He points to a glass box with a door on either end. "Step in here. You will feel three blasts of air. After the third blast, wait until the light turns green and walk out. Meet me at that table." He points to a stainless steel table. Somehow, my duffel bag is already on the table and an older man wearing blue latex gloves is waiting for me. I do as I am told. After the light turns green, I sit on a flimsy office chair, shoeless, still holding my doctor's note. The two men stand on the other side of the table with their hands behind their backs.

"Ask her what's in the bag," says the older man.

"What's in the bag?" says the younger security officer.

"It's two jugs of urine for a drug trial at OHSU," I say. "It has to be refrigerated. I have a doctor's note." I try to show him the note.

The old man waves my hand away with a dismissive frown. He mumbles something in the young man's ear. The younger security officer opens up my bag and digs out the green cooler with my urine in it. From somewhere he produces a white square of paper—or is it cloth? I can't tell. He takes the white square and runs it along the seam of the zipper. His hands are shaking. I realize this must be a training so I just sit there trying to appear non-threatening. Neither of them are looking at me, anyway. I want to ask what the white cloth is, but decide against it.

I listen to the thudding of the plastic bins. The machine hasn't skipped a beat. Travelers keep streaming by. The whole apparatus keeps beeping and sludging along. The white cloth disappears just as quickly as it appeared.

"Do a visual check," says the old man.

"What?"

"Visual check," he says.

The young security officer unzips the collapsible cooler with his shaky hands and ever so slightly peeks inside. The older man scrambles to get a view of the two opaque jugs of my urine. I'm getting slightly annoyed now—I went through all the trouble to make sure my urine was nice and cold for the lab and here they are leaking all that cold air out into the sweaty San Francisco airport. The old man smiles and looks at me for the first time. "Well, we've seen blood and a lot of other stuff—but never urine."

And then, as if by magic, they're gone. They don't even bother to zip up my bag. I stand and look around. With the note still in hand, I find my shoes and purse, then cram the cooler back into my duffel bag and make my way to the gate.

Signs and Signals

I CAN'T STOP SMOKING. I know it's addictive, but lately I've been a chimney. I've been buying whatever is cheapest. I made the mistake of buying two packs of Pall Mall Oranges and burned through them in no time. They were disgusting. I kept waiting for the nicotine to kick in. It never did.

My skin feels like it's got ants running around all over it. The muscles around my shoulders scream at me. My throat feels like a dried-out accordion. In the mornings, I wheeze. I wake up in the middle of the night picking my nose.

There are signs and signals if you keep your wits about you. All the convenience store owners have started telling me how bad cigarettes are for me. Now I know I'm in trouble. The Greek guy down Chenery Street has stopped trying to pressure me into purchasing his homemade baba ganoush and hummus and just silently shakes his head when I buy my smokes. The storeowner on the corner of Mission and Richmond asks me if my metal canteen is coffee. "Oh, no," I say after sucking the nozzle until it moans. "This is my water. I've already had enough coffee this morning."

"You've got to drink water after coffee," he says, picking up his own mug. "It's good for you to stay hydrated. These, on the other hand," he says, shoving two packs of ultra-light Fortunas across the counter, "are not good for you."

I give him a sheepish smile. I want to ask him when he plans to put his foot down and stop selling me these things. I open the pack and hand him the foil wrapper and barely make it out the front doors before I light up. Today I will drink four cups of coffee, a latte, a can of Coke, and nearly seven glasses of water. I can't stop peeing. At 9:00 p.m. tonight my kidneys hurt so bad I can't concentrate and have to leave class early. It finally occurs to me that I forgot to take my half pill of Desmopressin this morning—the hormone that helps my body retain water.

I have a coupon to Office Max. I'm wheeling my red metal cart down Folsom to see what kind of deals they have. I pass a parking lot rimmed by a tangled chain-link fence. Against a brick wall a man rests on the ground, reading the newspaper and talking to himself. His shopping cart is blue and covered in a blue tarp. He wears a blue jacket and a blue stocking cap. The sun is about to set and the light brings out the beautiful colors in his clothes ...

I keep pushing my cart down 16th Street. It's started to sprinkle and water creeps up the cuffs of my jeans, which are dragging on the ground. Even with a belt I can't seem to find pants that fit me properly. I'm wearing an old red wool Eagle-Scout jacket, fuzzy with pills. I'm wearing slip-on rubber shoes, and a red-checkered hat that is too big for me and sticks a good four inches off my head. I've convinced myself that worrying about my appearance is a waste of time and brain space. That space in my brain is better used for remembering to take my medications: my antidepressant, my antianxiety, my painkillers—but of course after a while I can't remember how many of those I've taken, either. And I'm not sure if that's even a proper metaphor for the brain, anyway—as if it was a filing cabinet with limited space—a closed system.

This morning I woke up with the "America" song from *West Side Story* stuck in my head. I think I go back to San Juan, I know a boat you can get on. Bye bye. Over and over and echoing.

I'm almost to the office supply store. I'm going to buy some folders and decorate them with dried flowers and pictures of chimpanzees so I can sell them on the Internet. I have to make some money if I'm going to be able to stay in San Francisco over the summer. I duck my soggy hat under the now dripping branches of some cherry trees. Suddenly, the front wheels of my cart get jammed up on a curb and I almost go over the handles. It occurs to me that I might be mentally ill.

My grandma and I are sitting in the front seat of her car. We've just had lunch and she is dropping me off at my parents' house. "I want to pray with you," she says.

Over our lunch, egg salad for her, chicken salad for me, I told her that I'd be fine with that. What harm could it do? I'm not a believer, not in prayer, anyway. I don't think God sits up there like the governor of Texas going over parole board documents, pardoning some and not others. But I do know that this prayer will make her feel better, like she's actually doing something for me. This is the way she shows her love, and receiving that love is pleasant. I'm not sure if this whole experience of being sick, of going through two failed brain surgeries, a failed drug study, and dare I say it, as much suffering as Jesus, has made me any more spiritual, but it has made me more superstitious.

"Okay," I say.

My grandma takes a small glass bottle out of her purse and unscrews the black plastic cap. She tips it over. As I guessed, it's some kind of ceremonial oil. She pauses, the oil glistening on the tip of her small, manicured index finger.

"I was at church last week," she says, "and God gave me a vision for you. It just came out of nowhere. In the vision I punched you in the stomach as hard as I could and a tumor the size of an egg came out of your mouth. It was yellow and it had purple veins all intertwined in it. Then it just rolled down your belly. It's obvious. God is going to heal you. You will be healed."

She takes some of the oil and lightly presses it to my forehead. "God, we pray for healing for Martha. And we *know* that you will heal her. Amen."

"Okay," I say, trying to get the image of my grandmother's tiny fist punching my bloated stomach out of my mind.

"I would like to pray now," I say, and I take my grandmother's hands in mine, resting them on top of the cup holders between us. I close my eyes. I know that this is part of the ritual, that you have to close your eyes. "Dear God, I pray for calm these days, I pray for calm and peace and acceptance for my family and myself for whatever is to come. And I pray for no fear for my family and myself. Amen."

My grandmother squeezes my hands. "Amen," she says, and screws the cap back on her oil. She looks up at me, satisfied. "Fear is the opposite of faith," she says.

I know she wants a response but for some reason my mind goes blank. I have nothing to say to that. "What kind of oil is that?" I ask, changing the subject.

"I don't know," she says. "I got it at Christian Supply. I love the way it smells." She takes off the cap and puts it under my nose like it's smelling salts.

I can't smell anything. "Mmm," I say. "That's nice."

Swedish Massage

AFTER WE'VE DECIDED on a time for my one hour, $30 Swedish massage, and the massage therapist gives me directions to her house, she tells me how much I'm going to love the massage, you're going to love this Martha, she says, it'll be amazing, and then in a couple days I drive to the massage therapist's house and park across the street, and I realize her house is a weekly hotel, the Railroad Hotel, and she meets me outside on the sidewalk in front of the locked front door in her nurse scrubs, because after all, it said on the coupon my roommate gave me that she was a registered nurse, and I smile, relieved to have found the place because I am new to San Francisco and got a little lost on the way over, and then we walk up two flights of stairs and down a hallway past a skinny older man and a sign on the wall, underlined in red, telling tenants not to throw their hypodermic needles in the trash, and I smell fish and the massage therapist says that someone is cooking something disgusting, and I follow her into her room where there is no massage table, only a double bed and a massage chair and a microwave and a cardboard chart of the acupressure points of the human body tacked to the wall, and the massage therapist tells me to take off all my clothes and sit down on the chair, and asks me whether I've ever had a chair massage before and I tell her I haven't and she tells me that I'm just going to love it and to take off all my clothes and put them on that chair and she points to a chair against the wall next to a dying palm tree and I tell her that I need to use the bathroom and she frowns and hands me a roll of toilet paper and shows me down the hall where the bathroom is and tells me this is why the massage is only $30, and I lock the door behind me and pee, and walk back to the room and realize I forgot the toilet paper next to the toilet, but the massage therapist is waiting for me and tells me to take off all my clothes and get into the massage chair next to the floor-to-ceiling windows and that I'm going to love this massage, and she asks me if I've ever had acupressure before and I say no and she tells me that I'm going to love it, that it will work wonders for tension and to take off all my clothes, and so I take off my clothes right there in the too-bright room while she watches me and I put them on the chair, everything except for my underwear, which I keep on, and I sit down on the cold vinyl massage chair, with my scarred, white belly hanging over the elastic waistband of my underwear and onto my knees, and I shiver because it's a little cold in the room, and the massage therapist tells me to stick my head down in the headrest and asks me if I'm comfortable and I say no not really and she adjusts the headrest and asks me am I comfortable now and I say no and she says, "Why not?"

Alphabet Soup

AT THE CUSHING'S CONFERENCE over the weekend, Dr. K told me that Dr. N was not qualified to perform my third brain surgery. I might have to sue my insurance company, he said. So I went home and e-mailed Dr. C and asked him about it. I asked him if I should see Dr. L, because Dr. K had also recommended her as a great doctor and someone with whom I might get a good second opinion. Dr. C wrote me back that Dr. N was a good and qualified surgeon and that if I wanted I could make Dr. L my primary care endocrinologist. So I went to see Dr. L, who knew Dr. K and had spoken to Dr. C and reassured me that not only was Dr. N qualified, but that my adrenal surgeons Dr. B and Dr. G were the "dream team." So I went home reassured, at least, that my adrenal surgeons, Dr. B and Dr. G, were qualified to remove my organs. I woke up this morning to a voice-mail from Dr. K, stating that he wasn't qualified to write a letter to my insurance company stating that Dr. N was not qualified unless I became his patient and he reviewed my files and was able to review Dr. N's outcomes and surgery history. This made sense to me. I considered calling Dr. W up in Portland to see if she was willing to write me a letter about Dr. N. But I guess I'll cross that bridge when I come to it. So today I have to go get some labs drawn at the medical center in San Francisco before I see Dr. Z and Dr. X on Friday so that they can run two tubes up my groin and into my brain.

March 12, 2010
9:00 a.m.

I'VE BEEN GIVEN a glossy advanced care directive packet in surgical admitting. I've signed the papers telling me about the risks of this surgery—that I may have a stroke, get an infection, that I may not wake up. Now I'm sitting on the hospital bed in a gown, reciting the list of my current medications to my fidgety nurse. Mike and Rachael, my younger brother and sister, sit in plastic hospital chairs ten feet away. None of us have had breakfast or coffee. Mike sits with his head in his hands, elbows on knees. Rachael stares open-mouthed at the floor, her gauzy vintage dress making a ghostly shadow on the white hospital tiles.

"You're taking insulin?" asks the nurse, pecking at the keyboard.

"I've never taken insulin."

The nurse, a thin older woman in purple scrubs, keeps surreptitiously stuffing pistachios from a ziplock bag into her mouth. "How about Synthroid?"

"I'm not taking any Synthroid. What else? Metformin—"

"Wait." The nurse holds up her hand. "I'm not to that part yet." She pokes at the keyboard and looks up at the computer screen through her bifocals. Keyboard, patient, screen—her head bobs back and forth, back and forth.

My frustration with her bubbles up through the murk of Norco,

Ativan, and Lexipro I've already taken this morning. I am staring up at the silver curtain rings.

The nurse furrows her brows. Prompted by something on the computer screen, she asks if I understand the procedure I am about to have. "Or do you want me to explain it to you?" she says.

I have a pretty good idea of what this sinus sampling is all about. In fact, I've gone through it once before. IPSS. Inferior Petrosal Sinus Sampling. The surgeons make two incisions on either side of my groin and run catheters up my veins into the pituitary cavern in the center of my brain, behind my nose, and take samples of the hormones the gland secretes. But face-to-face with a qualified individual, I can't resist. She might have more information, something new to add. And who am I kidding—there's a kind of satisfaction in testing her. In listening to the surgery explained in all its grotesque specificity.

"Sure," I say, smoothing down my hospital gown.

The nurse blinks at me, as if I'm the first person to ever take her up on this offer.

"Okaaay," she says. "Well," she says, "the doctors will be taking five samples overall in certain timed increments." She takes an impatient breath. "I think every five minutes? We will make one incision on the left side and two—yes, I think—two incisions on the right side. We stimulate you with hormones and then we take out those samples ... and we put them on ice in different containers. Five containers, I think." The nurse looks at me in disbelief. "Do you really want to hear all of this?"

"Yes," I say.

Rachael asks me if I want them to stay for all of this.

I look from her, to Mike, to my annoyed nurse. The nurse is trying to explain a procedure that she keeps calling an angiogram even though I know that's not what we are doing. She keeps calling it a cerebral angiogram. What is that? At the same time she keeps asking me if I'm currently in pain and how I would rate it. I tell her my feet hurt and my knees hurt and my hip hurts and my hands hurt. And she keeps saying, "Wait, wait, where is your pain?" And pecking at the keyboard. A large blonde nurse walks in and sets her purse down hurriedly in a corner. She apologizes for being late and starts to ask the skinny nurse how the skinny nurse's visit with her mom went. The skinny nurse says, "When she's not around, you know, it's out of my mind. I don't even think about her. But then when it's right in your face like that—it's like—" she takes a step back from the monitor and lets out a big sigh. "I know she's dying." She looks down at me. "Where is your pain?"

Another nurse walks in and hears me say that I am allergic to intravenous iodine dye. She looks annoyed and starts asking me what the allergic reaction was. "A rash," I say.

"Dermal. Did you ever have allergic reactions to shellfish?"

"I don't like shellfish," I say. "I never really ate it when I was a kid."

"No crab? No lobster?"

"Not really," I say.

"Well," the nurse says, "we may have to give you steroids."

"I don't want steroids," I say. "I have Cushing's. I have enough steroids already."

The skinny nurse is still pecking away the computer. "You were diagnosed with Cushing's in late 2007. What was the first symptom? Weight gain?"

"Osteoporosis."

"I have to go to a meeting," the other nurse says. She looks at me and then at the fidgeter. "Be sure to tell Dr. Collins about the iodine."

The skinny nurse takes another handful of pistachios and looks over at Rachael and Mike. "You guys don't need to be here for all of this. You can go wait in the waiting room. We'll call you."

Rachael gets up and gives my hand a squeeze. "Good luck, Martha. We love you."

Mike rubs some sleep out of his eyes. "Love you Marth. We'll see you in a bit."

And then they are gone.

The nurse watches Mike and Rachael pick up their things and walk out of the room. She squints back at the computer. "You're sure brave to let them leave," she says, and crunches down on a nut. The anesthesiologist comes in and introduces himself. The nurse starts to put my IV in. "I understand you've had this procedure before," he says, smiling at me. "You're a veteran!"

"I should get a medal or something," I say.

The nurse presses down hard into my vein. She is asking me to make a fist.

I want my brother and sister to come back and hold my hand. I am not brave. I am not brave at all. What the hell? Am I going straight into surgery?

The anesthesiologist puts a hand on my shoulder. "Are you okay?" he says.

I shake my head and fight back the tears.

"After this you'll be an old pro," he says. "Now don't look at her putting that needle in. I'm going to give you a sedative."

And he starts telling me how I have Cushing's Disease and how I've had two surgeries already and all this other stuff both of us already know, but he is smiling so big that I am able to pretend that he's telling me a fairy tale.

(Optional Supplement)

Personal Health Care Instructions Communication Form
Name: MARTHA GROVER

I. How much do I want to know about my condition:
(Please mark statement 1 or 2.)

1: I wish to know all relevant facts about my condition. I can cope better with what I know than with the unknown.

2: I do not wish to know all the details of my condition, especially if the news is bad. I fear that such knowledge will lessen my will to live and will cast a shadow over the time left to me. If there is bad news about my condition, I want my health care agent to take over making medical decisions for me, even if I still have mental capacity to make health care decisions myself.

Fathom

I AM LISTENING to the radio and they just announced that the plastic gyre, the floating isle of trash in the Pacific Ocean, is the size of Texas. Earlier today, I heard that the floods in Australia cover an area roughly the size of Texas. Now I'm wondering why, why has Texas become the measure of catastrophe, the benchmark of big? As big as what? As big as my joy, as big as my fear? As big as big? And then I wonder—just how big is Texas? Exactly how big are we talking? And I realize, what I don't know about Texas would cover an area roughly the size of Texas.

But what about what I do know? I do know—that if all the universe were the size of a football stadium and the earth were a golf ball, and if you took the cells in my body and laid them end to end, and if you made each entry in the Encyclopedia Britannica the size of a period on this page, they would either fit in the palm of my hand or they would fit through the eye of a needle or they would go all the way to the moon and back.

All I Really Know About Texas is that I remember you when you moved from Austin to Olympia, Washington, and we went to school together there in concrete buildings with oppressive lighting. You spent the first three months raving about how glad you were not to be in Texas anymore. But two months into Olympia's suicidal, irreverent winter, after nights begging rides to Seattle for punk shows, after rejections and faux-pas, you turned nineteen and got a simple outline tattoo, the size of a butterfly, a tattoo of Texas on your upper arm. As if to admit that this was a piss-poor substitute for the real thing, but that at least you could still remember where you came from. And after that you fell in love with my roommate who flew from Santa Cruz with two bongs in her duffel bag. And I moved and never saw you again.

And now, seconds later, they're announcing that the size of the gyre has actually been vastly exaggerated. It's not as big as they originally thought. We can all breathe a sigh of relief: the actual size is closer to Rhode Island. Closer to Hawaii, closer to some other small thing, a huggable state, closer to something you can wrap your arms around, something you can fathom.

Rotisseries

LISA AND I end up at Chopsticks to sing karaoke. I sing "Helter Skelter." She sings "Regulator." A douche bag with a braided pony-tail hits on me. Later, the guy who does "The Humpty Dance" asks her to come and sit at his table. We decline. The KJ does "Rapper's Delight" as a closing act. We stay until they kick us out. Lisa and I ride our bikes home and stumble into my apartment. As usual, my roommate is at her boyfriend's house. I tell Lisa she can sleep in my roommate's bed. I give her some pj's. We turn off the lights. From my futon I tell her that I don't have the spins, I have the "slowly rotatings."

"You're like a chicken," she calls back.

"What?"

"You're like a hot dog."

"Yeah," I laugh. "I don't have the spins. I have the rotisseries."

In the morning, I stumble down to the coffee shop to write. The barista with the neck tattoo tells me I look grumpy. "I'm hungover," I say.

When I leave, I tell him to take it easy and he says see you round man.

I hate it when boys call me man.

Boy 1

He sits next to me at the coffee shop talking about Hong Kong. From where I'm sitting, I can see through his irises—the lightest blue, almost transparent, as though his eyeballs were made of water, of weak blue tea. He's lived in Hong Kong for two years. We sit in the North Portland coffee shop, all hot and humid in the cold winter afternoon. "In Hong Kong," he says, "you can walk for miles through overhead, glass-enclosed passages. You never have to walk on the street if you don't want to."

Boy 2

I have stress fractures in my ankles but I don't know it yet—I think I have tendonitis. I'm dating someone who's ashamed of his hairy back yet criticizes my abundant pubic hair. I limp around the grocery store where I work in the cheese department. At 8:00 a.m., I roll my cart loaded with Feta, fresh Mozzarella, and sliced Gouda out to the stand-up case to stock the morning cheese. I lean on the cart like it's a walker. The lanky perishable-grocery assistant manager is stocking the commodity cheeses. He looks up and asks why I'm limping. "I have tendonitis," I say.

He gives me a sympathetic smile. "I've been studying energy work," he says. (He's in school for holistic medicine and massage.) "Our bodies are like batteries. They have positive and negative poles. For example, if I touched you here," he indicates my ankle, "and then you touched me here," he indicates his neck, his shoulders, his head, his hair, "it would create a circuit of positive and negative energy flowing through our bodies." I don't say anything.

Boy 3

He is shorter than me. Much shorter. He pulls on his cigarette and doesn't inhale. "I think I have cancer," he says. *I have cancer, too,* I think. I lose my virginity to him.

Boy 4

He approaches me in the courtyard of the community college and asks to draw my picture in exchange for a cigarette. I agree.

"Hey, that looks just like you." I say when he's done.

"Yeah, I know. That's all I can draw. Everything just ends up looking like a drawing of myself."

"Here's a cigarette."

"Thanks."

Boy 4 again

Four years later he calls me up out of the blue and asks me if I want to go get a drink with him. I've just graduated from college and am working at the restaurant where I'd worked before I went to school. He's been fired from his job as a janitor at the funeral home. "Why did they fire you?" I ask.

"My boss made this action at me, just joking, like he was gonna shoot me. You know, with his arms. I told him I didn't think that was very funny. It really scared me. You know, you just shouldn't joke about things like that. He thought I was overreacting so he fired me."

"Are you still painting?"

"No."

But he still lives with his strange, disapproving parents in a cul-de-sac near the lake. It's dark when I pull up. When my headlights hit the front bay window he comes out, pulling a thin, tan jacket up over his gray T-shirt. He jumps into the passenger seat and closes the door. "Pull around the corner here," he says, pointing around the corner of his house, towards the backyard.

He still hasn't looked me in the eye. I size him up. He's gained what looks like a lot of water-weight. His hair is greasy.

"Just pull around the corner here. I need to get my beer."

"I thought that's what we're doing. We're gonna get a drink."

"I don't have any money. I have some beer hiding around the corner here, behind the shed." He points and makes a whirly motion with his index finger.

"Why don't I just buy you a drink?"

"I have all this beer already. How many beers do you want to buy me?" He keeps pointing.

I feel weird now. Sitting in the driveway with my lights on and motor running. I pull slowly out of the driveway.

"I really don't care," I say. "Besides, where are you going to drink them? In the car?"

He ignores me and keeps pointing to the backyard. "I'll just run and get them. You drive the car away from the block and then stop and I can run back and get them, so they don't see."

"Why are you hiding beer outside?"

"My parents don't like me drinking."

I'm driving my car very slowly now. "Why not?"

"It makes the medication I'm taking stop working." He's looking out through the dark window at the backyard. His nose is so close to the glass it's almost touching.

"What medication are you on?"

"Anti-psychotics." His breath fogs up the window.

"Oh."

"Just go around the corner here." He still hasn't said hi or looked me in the eye. He keeps staring out the window.

Boy 5

I'm still limping around with my stress fractures. He calls me and asks me if I want to meet him at the Powell's downtown for coffee. I limp to the bus station and make it all the way downtown. I'm grouchy and in pain. I wait for twenty minutes in the crowded coffee shop and when he shows up, he sits down and shoves his chair sideways, slightly away from me. He looks over my shoulder and sits with his body facing halfway away from me. We exchange small talk until he starts to tell me about the bug that flew into his ear and died. He was on his bike and it flew into his ear. His immediate reaction was to slap the side of his face. This action killed the bug inside his ear and he'd recently had to go to the doctor to have it removed.

"Do you want to see it?" he asks.

"Of course."

He pulls a piece of tissue out of the breast pocket of his jean jacket and carefully unfolds it. I examine the remains; it's hard to tell exactly what species of bug it is, as smashed as it is.

"I think it means something. That this happened," he says, placing the bug carefully back into his pocket with a nod.

"What do you mean?"

"That my first reaction was to kill the bug. I think it means I should stop eating meat again."

"You think you killed the bug because you eat meat now?"

"It was my first instinct—to kill the bug."

"It flew into your ear while you were biking."

"But I don't think I would've done that had I still been a vegetarian."

"When I pour out my little fish tank to clean it out, my goldfish's first instinct is to swim against the current—even though what I'm doing is for his benefit. We can't help our instincts."

He just stares at me. The conversation is over. He asks me if I want to go see *Jackass: The Movie*.

"No. I don't want to go see that movie."

He walks and I limp down to the Mexican restaurant attached to the back of the strip club. He orders a burrito and I order a beer.

If I remember correctly, he talks about his new cat for the rest of our time together, and then I leave.

Boy 6

I'm lying in bed with an engineer. Last night, over beer, he told me about his job. "My job involves making curves in roads so that everyone is comfortable. Like if someone is driving along a bridge I've built they won't get that "roller coaster" effect. Their stomach won't flip flop. I make the curve as steep as possible without that happening—so people can drive as fast as possible without feeling sick. If people feel sick it doesn't mean their speed is unsafe, per se, but it does mean they'll immediately slow down, which will impede the steady flow of traffic."

"Your job is to make the road as dangerous as possible?"

"Yeah," he says. "Basically."

Nice White Girls

BECAUSE IT'S FRIDAY NIGHT and we're young and have a few more pennies in our pockets, Lisa and I head over to the Paragon on Albina and Killingsworth for karaoke.

The Paragon, according to Lisa, usually has karaoke on the weekends. She's excited because she's been practicing "Words of Love" by The Mamas & the Papas. We arrive and are buzzed in through the iron gate. The bar is divided into two rooms and we can hear loud music coming from the back room. We get our drinks and make our way back to the karaoke area.

Instead of karaoke, there is a punk quartet. The drummer, shirtless and tattooed, wears a red bowler hat. The lead singer has on an American flag, his head poking through a hole. On top of his head he wears an army helmet. Lisa and I claim a booth, smile at each other, shrugging. Here we are, karaoke-less. But, we have to admit, the band is kind of entertaining. They have passion—the redeeming factor in any and all punk music. An older black man in a trench coat and stocking cap sits in a booth near the front and plays an enthusiastic air guitar, periodically pausing to punch the air with his hands.

He's the only black person in the room. Not unusual in Portland, but a bit of a surprise in this neighborhood. Everyone else seems to be friends of the band. I wonder if ten years ago this would've been the case, if there would've been a punk band playing here. If there would've been any white kids in this neighborhood at all.

The band finishes their set and says their thank yous. The old man gets up all jerky-kneed and shouts, his finger in the air. "One more! Just one more!"

Everyone cheers. I hoot. And so, with gusto, the band launches into another song. The old man now struts around the stage with his air guitar, half-participant, half-observer. He bangs on his imaginary drum and drops into a chair to nod his head. Soon he begins pantomiming the lead singer—punk vocalist as interpreted by a drunk 70-year-old.

As the last notes of the song ring through the air, the old man screams, "One more! One more for the people! *For the people!*"

Lisa and I laugh. He really seems genuine. He's clearly having a better time than the rest of us.

But I can't help but wonder who *the people* are. There are certainly none of his people present. And when I think about it, none of my people here, either. I suddenly feel very isolated.

No one in the audience backs him up as he pleads for an encore, but the band is listening. The lead singer breathes into the mic, "We'll take it that this guy speaks for everybody."

Repeat this scene three times.

By the end of it, the old man has his arm draped around the lead singer's neck and is shouting into the mic, "That's a wrap folks! That's a wrap!" As the band breaks down their equipment, the old man makes the rounds, shaking hands and shouting that he loves that "hard rock!" And that he can't hear a "goddamn thing" and that he hates "opera." But the white kids are laughing nervously. Some of them even wave him away as he approaches their booths.

Lisa and I chat a while longer and decide that karaoke is out of the question now. We go out to the car. An older blonde woman is standing in front of the new wine bar next door smoking a cigarette. Lisa and I are still laughing and smiling as we get into the car.

"Where are you two going?" the woman shouts at us. "You should come in here for a drink!"

"We just had a drink," I say. "We're going home."

"Come on," the woman says, "we need some nice white girls like you in here."

I'm in the car by the time she says this. "What did she just say?" I ask Lisa, as I put the car in first and turn on the headlights.

"She called us nice white girls."

"That's what I thought." I concentrate on getting my car pointed south, back towards Lisa's house in northeast. The woman's figure recedes into the night, all smoke and paunch, pink cotton, black leather and bad dye job. "What's going on in this town?" I ask.

Lisa laughs. "Yeah, I mean, how does she know we're *nice?*"

Fifteen Things
I'm Not Putting
On My
OK Cupid Profile

1. THIS MORNING I put my iPod on shuffle, and strangely, the first two songs I heard were both about murdering women. The first was Tom Jones' "Delilah" and the second was Neil Young's "Down by the River." I prefer the Neil Young song.

2. I'm trying to come up with good evolutionary theories as to why men go bald or women live beyond menopause. Also—why is pleasure so often coupled with pain? So we can remember who we had sex with? My theory is that pain is the only way our brain remembers anything. More pain, more wrinkles on the brain. This makes sense—it's why we don't often eat nails. Or at least not enough nails to kill us.

3. When I was eight or nine, I used to sit alone in my room and gag myself. The reflex was what fascinated me. Just by sticking my index finger far enough down my throat, I could make my body do something it didn't want to do. It was as if I had taught myself to fly.

4. Parts of me perform irreconcilable actions. I have no control over these different parts.

5. A friend lives next door to an annoying, barking dog. I was over at this friend's house last week and we were drinking wine in his beautiful, plant-filled backyard. As the sun went down, the dog next door began barking.

"You hear that?" he asked. "Tomorrow morning, when my neighbors leave, or maybe even tonight, after they go to bed, I'm going to throw this over the bushes into their yard." He grabbed a paper bag from his feet and opened it up. Inside was a huge hunk of black forest ham, as big as his head. He explained that the dog would feast on the ham and then "puke and shit all over the inside of their house."

6. What makes me happy: Elton John. What makes me sad: Elton John singing about his wife.

7. When I am lonely, I think about George. How we hiked to the top of Latourel Falls together and sat down on the late summer sweet-smelling grass, and he leaned on one elbow, and I was on a rolled-up flannel, and we stared out at the Columbia River Gorge. His beard was the color of the golden grass. Little bugs began to land on our heads. I took a piece of plant and bent it over and over in my hands, until it was a lopsided square. I told him how I had hurt many people through my writing. And he asked me if I was sorry, 'cause I didn't sound like it. And I said nothing, just smiled at him.

Then he told me how he had kidnapped someone once. How he and his friend drove this guy around the block in their car, how they'd told this guy he better pay their mutual friend the money he owed, or else. George said he's lucky he's not in jail. And I thought, looking at him and smiling, how I'd prefer to be silent always, or else have conversations like these.

8. I am sad that even the removal of an organ is not enough to scare me into being responsible. Nor the threat of poverty, loneliness, disgust, despair, social stigma—none of it is heavy enough to make me endure unendurable boredom. I don't know how. I don't know how to do it.

9. What appeals to me is walking into the sea. I'd rather choose an outfit from my closet, get on the bus, get off the bus, walk to the edge of the ocean, my favorite place, and keep walking. Eventually, against my body's will, its fight to survive, one system will override the other, my mouth will burst open, water will fill my lungs and that will be it.

10. She said her friend made art and this had something to do with me. And I looked this friend up on the Internet. I didn't really understand the art. But I knew that yes, it did have to do with me, in some indescribable way. I just wasn't sure how. Her art was just a bunch of stuff falling apart, lying on the floor, in a gallery. Dressers, and lamps, and trash bags, and huge papier-mâché asses. And people were taking pictures, people were writing reviews. The artist, she is getting grants. I imagine my own parents drowning in trash.

11. When I was six or seven I secretly took the embroidery supplies upstairs into my room. After I got bored trying to follow the nursery rhyme patterns, I took the needle and punctured the heel of my left hand. The skin was thick and tough. I hardly felt a thing. I pulled the thread through. You could see the orange thread beneath the top layer of my skin, like my skin was lace or tracing paper. After that I poked each of my five fingers and pulled the thread through until my hand looked like it had been visited by a spider, or my hand had decided to throw a party and put up streamers, or it was involved in some torturous version of cat's cradle.

I didn't think anything was necessarily wrong with this behavior, but I had the nagging sensation that Mom would be upset if she caught me. Similar to the reaction I received when I was caught sucking on my baby sister Zoe's earlobes and toes. "Martha!" my mother cried. "You don't suck on other people's toes! If you want to suck on a body part, suck on your own body part!"

I was ashamed, but mostly I thought it was unfair. My own toes were dirty and smelled bad, and my mind briefly puzzled over how I might suck on my own earlobe. In defiance, I took to picking my own scabs. Just a little. Just around the edges. Just so that they would bleed a little bit. Sometimes I would get carried away and tear off a big chunk. And then I would bleed a lot. I liked the way the blood was so deeply red and then how it turned brown when it dried. It reminded me of my wet footprints on hot concrete—how satisfying it was to watch them evaporate. As if I were invisible, as if I were disappearing.

Inevitably, Mom would find me with blood running down my leg and I would have to admit I had done it myself. But I didn't mind too much—it meant that Mom would sit me up on the counter in the bathroom and swab my scab with hydrogen peroxide. I liked to watch it fizz. I enjoyed the burning sensation. It reminded me of the time I drank some cough syrup, and it burned and warmed my whole body. Mom watched the fizzing too for a while, all spaced out, one hand on my knee, just the two of us together. Then she snapped out of it and told me to stop picking my scabs for God's sake.

13. I watch that show *The Dog Whisperer*. Like, a lot. On the show, Cesar Milan often describes his dog training techniques through the use of analogy. For example, if the client with the misbehaving dog is a plumber, he will use plumbing analogies. If the client is an art collector, he will say something like, "Well, your dog has certainly made his own work of art by peeing on your carpet." This

approach seems to work well; you can see the light bulb go on in people's faces that they finally "get" what he is talking about. But if you're not the Dog Whisperer—don't do this. It's fucking condescending.

14. A lot of people ask the question: if you could only have one album, forever, on a desert island, what would it be? I'm more interested in what I would be wearing. I think of old military clothes— shirts and jackets and old cargo pants, their skin as soft and velvety as sand. Look, I was a kid once, with a loincloth, a bead necklace, a rattle. I know what it is to be sentimental.

15. I used to date skinny men. I mean really skinny, so skinny and tall they looked as if they were walking into a strong wind, men that had hipbones like daggers, who had to eat every hour on the hour or they would fall over from exhaustion. And now I see a love handle, bulging over a belt, skimming the surface of a flimsy T-shirt, and it doesn't make me think, as I used to, that someone's let himself go. It's just, as far as I'm concerned, a way the body tells you that yes, I am here. This is where I'm at, just checking in.

I'd like to thank my family, Caroline Goodwin, Shanthi Sekaran, all my subscribers, my friends from Portland and CCA, and John Dovydenas.

Hello! I am a 29 year-old single woman living in San Francisco looking for a man between the ages of 25 and 40. Some important facts about me: I have the exact same birthday as Lil Wayne. When I go camping, I like to be the one who builds the fire. My hair is brown. Today a checker at Trader Joe's noted that I brought my own bag and said I must be "responsible." I can think of almost no situations when I would be happy wearing socks to bed but also feel that people have the right to sleep in their socks if they want to. You should respond to this ad if you are a single dad, a farmer, you ride a bike and / or you call the Internet the "Monsternet."

flashlightmonster@gmail.com

Small-time art thug seeks someone soft to lean on during fits of hopelessness and childlike greed, will reciprocate. Currently working as a freelance journalist, artist, and part-time bike-part hustler. I'm 33 but act like an 18-year-old matured to the level of a half-sophisticated 23-year-old. Love cooking, long walks, reading books about reading books, and shoplifting things I don't like or want. Eager to hear from women whose friends and families are just a little worried, but not really, just sort-of. Never been arrested and proud. As far as looks are concerned, I am tall, built for petty theft, and bald. Looks aren't important but you should look like you're mean and short-fused and just a couple deep sighs from getting totally unhinged. Open-mindedness is essential, but if you like helmet-football go to hell right now, don't even look at me with those things. Whatever.

roderick.mcclain@gmail.com

HIGHLY DESIRABLE WOMAN AVAILABLE. Has lots of friends. Tall. Good hair. Exciting lifestyle. Frequents interesting places. Complimentary habits. Very engaging stories. Edifying personality. Good in the kitchen. Good at other things. Very entertaining at parties. Really generous at bars. Okay with computers and wi-fi. Pretty good with navigation. Excellent correspondent. Fair at general trivia. Above average at pop-culture trivia. Modest VHS collection. Could be better at dominos. Prefers to have a better time. Seeks a good man.

karnes.jordan@gmail.com

The other day a friend told me I have exciting thighs. That was nice to hear. And recently some hooligans reaffirmed that, indeed, I have a real mustache. Thanks guys! I am a 32-year-old male looking for a woman, details TBA. I'm known to sing Björk songs in the shower, never watch the road—nearly bike off bridges—and plan conceptual art soup dinners. Occasionally I mistake X-ACTO knives for pens. That's my picnic basket up there. I only partially made it. OTHER HIGHLIGHTS INCLUDE: totally not on Facebook // half-Mexican and half-Vietnamese // only in three unsuccessful Portland bands // fixed a pair of glasses with a chopstick and tape // wore them for a year // and am probably still 32 ... even when the book you're holding is a decade old

meximese@gmail.com

Martha Grover has a master's degree in creative writing from California College of the Arts. Her work has appeared in *The Coachella Review, Switchback, Broken Pencil, Never Have Paris Zine, Tom Tom Magazine, The Raven Chronicles,* and her zine *Somnambulist*, which she has been publishing since 2003. She lives in Portland, Oregon.

For more information about Martha and to subscribe to her zine, visit www.somnambulistzine.blogspot.com.

The Cushing's Support & Research Foundation is located online at www.csrf.net.